Exploring Texas History

Exploring Texas History

Weekend Adventures

ELAINE L. GALIT AND VIKK SIMMONS

A REPUBLIC OF TEXAS PRESS BOOK
TAYLOR TRADE PUBLISHING
Lanham • New York • Dallas • Toronto • Oxford

A REPUBLIC OF TEXAS PRESS BOOK

Published by Taylor Trade Publishing
An imprint of The Rowman & Littlefield Publishing Group, Inc.
4501 Forbes Boulevard, Suite 200
Lanham, Maryland 20706

Distributed by National Book Network

Library of Congress Cataloging-in-Publication Data

Galit, Elaine L.
    Exploring Texas history : weekend adventures / Elaine L. Galit and Vikk
Simmons.
        p. cm.
    Includes index.
    ISBN 1-58979-202-5 (pbk. : alk. paper)
    1. Texas—Guidebooks. 2. Historic sites—Texas—Guidebooks. 3. Texas—
History, Local. I. Simmons, Vikk. II. Title.
    F384.3.G35 2005
    917.6404'64—dc22

                                                            2004021275

Manufactured in the United States of America.

As always, to the joy in my life, my children and grandchildren, for their love and support. For my girls: Heidi Andrews, Shari Burrows, Lauri Coppock, Staci Andrews, Demi Andrews, Amanda (Mandi) Coppock, Marisa Burrows, and Brandi Burrows. And my guys: Randy Burrows, Jay Coppock, and Doug Coppock. May we continue to enjoy the treasure of our lives together. For my parents, Alma and Al Jacobs, who would have loved the journey.

. . . And for Ray, who would have been proud.

With Love,
Elaine

To my parents, who are always there. To Karen and Dustin, Kortney and Dylan, for the inspiration; to the boys—you know who you are—for the fun and laughter; to Deb, Karen, Heather, Jennifer, Charlotte, Lori, and Craig for your slightly bent ears; to Tracy F. and Evan F. for your support when needed; and to Michael Seidman, for your continued guidance. Thank you.

And for those who never knew, yet somehow did know: Nanny, Tommy, Mother Angie, and Jack. You are all remembered.

—Vikk

Contents

Preface

The Romance of Texas History

*When you want to read of excitement read the history of Texas.
It's mangy with romance.*

—*Will Rogers*

Every year during the month of August, the folks in the Panhandle town
of Higgins, Texas, celebrate Will Rogers Day. This twentieth-century hu-
morist dreamed of being a Texas cowboy, and he loved everything about
Texas. He loved the size of the state, and often jokingly compared the
buffalo wallows in Texas to the Lakes of Switzerland. Although funny, his
comparison ventures into the realm of possibility.

And possibility is what the Great State of Texas is all about. Even a cur-
sory look at Texas history shows that truth. Out of a virtual swamp, the
Allen brothers laid the foundation for a city that would become the fourth
largest in the United States. After losing a house through the devastation
of flood waters left by one of the many hurricanes that battle the Texas
Gulf Coast, one settler applied his shipmaking and engineering skills to
rebuild his house into one that would float. Despite the terrible loss of life
at the Alamo and the ensuing psychological punch, the small army of

Replica of early Texas poster. Vikk Simmons

Texas settlers chased after Santa Anna with such vengeance that in eighteen minutes, as if caught in a sea change, the world turned upside down, and the Texans defeated the Mexican army. Today the Alamo is a sacred site, a shrine to heroes honored and remembered the world over.

Anything is possible.

Possibility is the reason we wrote this book. We are curious. We are writers and we love stories. Texas is a big state with a history ripe with stories for the taking. Visiting the places where history has been made, watching reenactments, and listening to locals verify or hoot at tall tales are real treats. The state is so large that the range of stories and experiences

Texas Civil War reenactors during a Civil War Weekend at Liendo Plantation in Hempstead. Vikk Simmons

is truly vast, and, therefore, we cannot include them all. We hope the stories entertain, the history informs, and your curiosity will cause you to take a second look at that big, wide state begging for your exploration.

Mining even one layer of the state's history reveals a wealth of stories that speak to courage, heroism, and plain old front-porch storytelling. Visiting the settings, the wellspring of such stories, adds an extra dimension to the tales. Who can visit Liendo Plantation in Hempstead and not wonder whether the image of Elsabet Ney, dressed in Grecian robes and knee boots, will greet them just around the corner? How can a visit to the Alamo not cause your soul to grow quiet and hushed in the presence of such hallowed memories? And why are those restless, recurring, bobbing lights still teasing the visitors to Marfa?

The book is structured around the four major cities in Texas, plus the Texas Gulf Coast and the Panhandle–West Texas regions. History ranges from the early dinosaur years to the modern space age era. Piracy and maritime history, as well as the fight for independence and the Civil War are included, but many stories highlight the heroic pioneer and Wild West spirit that accompanied the waves of people that made up the state's immigration. In addition to a small overall history of the town or area, an adventure in history is plucked from the town's pages and re-told. Adventures continue with suggested places to eat and sleep.

Going to battlefields, farmhouses, log cabins, historic districts, land-marks, and markers, helps us connect with our past, and with the people who lived and died and fought there. In 1862, far away in a cornfield at Antietam, the Texas Brigade suffered immense losses. What made those men fight so far from home? The men and women who have made the great state of Texas have left a legacy that continues to fascinate the world. We hope this book leads you to discover the romance that is Texas.

Acknowledgments

This book would not exist without the help, inspiration, encouragement, and support from a great many people. Special thanks to Janet Harris for her editorial advice and to Rick Rinehart for his help during an unexpected transition.

We are also indebted to Mark Goodland for his airport runs; Adam Libarkin for his publicity input and invaluable e-mails; Ari Jacobs for her photographic advice; Michael Selewatch for his computer-guru advice; Mary Ann Colby for her support with Eli's mishugas; and Elaine Gladstone for always being there. Thanks to Congregation Or Ami and Jack Kronick for the wonderful bus trips to Palestine, Rusk, Goliad, and many other Texas towns.

Thanks to J. Z. Selewach who is always ready to hit the trails and particularly for the run-away-from-the-rain tour from College Station to Bandera. Special thanks to Dylan Hurst who eagerly submitted to a winter trip in search of dinosaur tracks, and to Gracie, John, and Joseph Greer for a great introduction to Dinosaur Valley. A special nod to Deb Whitaker, a friend indeed, who is always ready to help whenever asked.

Finally, our book is better for the help we received from the following people: Pam Fitch, Executive Director, Nacogdoches Convention and

Visitors Bureau; Sherry Nefford, Seguin Convention and Visitors Bureau; Dawn, Salado Chamber of Commerce; Russell Wright, Executive Director, Linden Economic Development Corp.; Doris Freer, member of the Goliad County Historical Commission and tour guide extraordinaire; Kelly Hamby of Surfside Beach; Wilfred Korth, Chief Ranger, Coleto Creek Park & Reservoir, Fannin; Johnny Calderon, Executive Director Marfa Chamber of Commerce; Rita Miller, Interim Executive Director, Port Lavaca–Calhoun County Chamber of Commerce and Agriculture; Robert Richardson, Matagordabay.com webmaster; Linda Wolff, Regional Coordinator, Texas Settlement Region; Nita Harvey, Poteet Strawberry Festival Association; Sondra from Marfa; April Allen, Tourism Director, Village of Salado; Elizabeth K. Trevino, Executive Assistant, Department of Public Information, City of Corpus Christi; Bradley Avant, Secretary, Gonzales Chamber of Commerce and Agriculture; Barbara Hand, Executive Director, Gonzales Chamber of Commerce and Agriculture; and Melissa Armstrong, Executive Director, Yorktown Chamber of Commerce.

1

Following Texas Trails

From the beginning, trails have crisscrossed the surface of Texas. Whether they're early trails made by Indians before the Spanish exploration or later trails made by cattle driving and railroads, the land has been a virtual road map. Today Interstate highways and city freeways add a new overlay.

The railroads could make or break a town, but before them came the rumbling wheels of stagecoaches across the state. Stagecoach inns followed. Some were mere log huts, but others were more elaborate. Dr. Frederick Roemer, a German scientist who wrote of his travels in his book *Texas* (1849), mentioned having to sleep on the floor of an attic. He wrote, "I had just captured a small mattress for my own use and had spread a thin cotton blanket over my chilly frame, when my host assigned another individual, utterly unknown to me, to share my bed and thin blanket with me." Although the inns once populated much of Texas, only a few still remain standing. The Fanthorp Inn, where Sam Houston once trained his troops in the front yard, is now in the Fanthorp Inn State Historic Park in Anderson, Texas. Two other well-known inns are deserving of visits: the Nimitz Hotel in Fredericksburg and San Antonio's Menger Hotel.

The Southern Overland Mail Route ran east to west, Sherman to Fort Quitman, through Texas, from 1858–1861. From Sherman, stop at Gainesville, Jacksboro, Fort Belknap, Fort Phantom Hill, Abilene, Fort Chadbourne, San Angelo, Fort Stockton, Fort Davis, Van Horn, and Quitman for a straight throughway. A couple of side trips will include visits to El Paso, the Piney and Pope's Camp, and the Panhandle-Plains Historical Museum to see an old stagecoach. The Butterfield Line of the Overland Mail Route didn't last long, only thirty-one months, but stage-coaches covered 2,750 miles of unbroken road. John Butterfield spent an entire year establishing the stations and the wells on the entire route before it could be opened.

Comanches, Kiowas, Apaches, and Lipan gave the early settlers plenty of problems, so the Texas forts were built to help provide military defense for the early Texas frontier. The Texas Historical Commission (THC) provides the Texas Forts Trail Region brochure. The brochures detail eight historic forts "where brave soldiers fought and lived more than one hundred years ago." There are many things to see, including a variety of battle reenactments and Indian pictographs on the bluffs in Paint Rock. The Texas Forts Trail is full of history. Some of the forts have living history weekends. Someone adventurous might take the route that runs from east to west and include Fort Richardson, Fort Belknap, Fort Griffin, Fort Phantom Hill, Fort Chadbourne, Fort Concho, Fort McKavett, and Fort Mason in his or her travels. Another might begin with Fort Bliss in El Paso and move to Fort Stockton, Fort Davis, Fort Leaton, Fort Lancaster, Fort Clark near Del Rio, and Fort Duncan.

The THC also offers the following travel guides: "Texas Independence Trail Region," "African Americans in Texas: Historical and Cultural Legacies," "Texas in the Civil War," and "Los Caminos del Rio: Legacies of the Borderlands." For a free copy of any brochure, contact 512-463-6255 (www.thc.state.tx.us). To learn about the Chisholm Trail and explore historic sites across the state, request the Chisholm Trail brochure.

For a different way of traveling across Texas, follow the restored County Courthouses. Most can be found within easy driving distance of San Antonio, Austin, and Dallas. In the early days, becoming a county was important in Texas life. The settlers had to have a completed 150-name petition, and the number wasn't always easy to reach. If you love architecture and are looking for some interesting photo captures, plan a trip that takes in the courthouses. The Denton County courthouse has several mixed architectural elements, while the 1930 Moore County courthouse in Dumas has eagle ornaments on its exterior. "Old Red" is Dallas County's famous courthouse. Wander up to Center, Texas, and see the 1885 Shelby County courthouse that has arches, turrets, and buttresses, all inspired by its Irish designer's homeland's castles.

For a glimpse into the grand life, plan a trip around the many historic hotels that call forth history and legend. San Antonio's Menger Hotel, Austin's Driskell, and Fort Worth's Stockyards Hotel are but a few. The historic Hotel Galvez is considered to be the first modern luxury resort in the state.

Sometimes the need to jump in the car and drive is overwhelming, or maybe a trip heading away from the rain and in the opposite direction of the thunderclouds is beckoning. Whatever the reason, driving tours are immensely popular in Texas. Many like to follow the old Route 66 and take in Cadillac Ranch along the way. Others go off in search of ghost towns by traveling from Marfa to Big Bend and taking in Plata, Presidio and the River Road, El Camino del Rio, then Lajitas, and so on. With the friendly Texas highway system, road trips are easy. For the dedicated road-tripper, a trip across the state using Interstate 10 is a must. Others like a less-than-straight-and-narrow approach and pick a state highway to zigzag their way across the countryside. Still others enjoy a tour down the Presidential Corridor to take in the LBJ Library in Austin, to the George Bush Presidential Library in College Station, and all points in between, or the Mission Corridor along the San Antonio River. If you don't like any of those, a tour down Highway 6 might provide some interesting side trips and could take you all the way to Oklahoma.

Finally, a trip through the Hill Country should be on every Texan's and every out-of-state visitor's hit list of things to do in Texas. Whatever your passion, Texas has just the right tour. Contact the Texas Historical Commission or take advantage of their fantastic website to help plan your next trip across the big state of Texas.

INDIANOLA: FOLLOW THE TRAIL

—— INDIANOLA, TEXAS ——

Imagine what it would be like to live in a dream city. In its heyday, Indianola, a bustling prosperous town on a beautiful harbor, was known as the Dream City of the Gulf.

Indianola began as Indian Point, nothing more than a piece of land that marked the oyster reef dividing Matagorda Bay from Lavaca Bay. In 1849 the seaport was renamed using the word Indian in combination

Texas Civil War campgrounds set up by reenactors.
Vikk Simmons

with the Spanish word for wave—ola. In 1853, the settlement at Powder-horn was incorporated as Indianola, leaving the original town site with the name Old Town. The townspeople flourished; but to overtake Galveston as the area's premier port, they knew they would have to build a railroad. Despite the intervention of the Civil War, the folks persevered, and the Indianola Railroad ran as far as Cuero. Less than two years later, at a time when the city was crowded with visitors, a terrible storm struck the port city. Nine hundred died and the place lay in shambles. After the 1875 storm, many moved their businesses and homes inland, but some tried to rebuild. Then, in 1880, another storm hit the city. In 1886 a third and final storm pounded Indianola, and the Dream City became a nightmare. In the aftermath the city had vanished, and the few people who did survive vowed never to return. The very sea that had created this vital port had destroyed her. These days Indianola is truly a "dream" city with a pink granite marker the only concrete reminder of its existence.

ADVENTURES IN HISTORY

Adventure was the name of the game, and men and women arrived at Indianola seeking a shorter route to the gold fields of California. From merchants to politicians, many eager to be where the action was, they streamed through the portals of the city. Ships left the port with silver from Mexico, beef hides, and even cattle, including the first beef carcasses carried to another port under refrigeration. However, in 1855 the U.S. War Department made the strangest use of the port when it hauled in at least two shipments of camels. The government planned an experiment: Would camels make better transports of military goods than horses or mules?

The first group of thirty-four camels, both one- and two-humped, arrived at Indianola in May 1856. Their destination was Camp Verde, and they made it there in August. During the fourteen months that one of the men, Amasa Clark, took care of the camels, he gathered enough camel hair from the shedding humps to make two camel hair pillows. Recently a treasure hunter at Camp Verde found a camel bell. Eventually the camels were used to map the Big Bend and the West Texas area. René-Robert Cavelier Sieur de La Salle of the failed Mississippi exploration, the French explorer who was so steeped in his own disaster, became the first to leave his footprints in the sands of Indianola. Today, this same man surveys the ghost town as a rose granite statue of himself that rises above the featureless sands.

ON THE MAP

The Indianola Trail begins in the Matagorda Bay area and goes inland all the way to New Braunfels.

WEEKEND ADVENTURES

Today Old Indianola is mostly under water, and all that is left is a pink granite stone near the historical marker. The marker is now on the shoreline of Matagorda Bay because of the erosion that moved the shoreline further inland.

According to Lone Star Internet—Texas Trails, "Today the tide laps at a few stones of the courthouse foundation. Inches above the smooth sand, outlines of a few shattered concrete cisterns remain. Some fishermen's homes have come of late, and the state has erected an historical marker." The trail, leading from the marker to New Braunfels, passes through many towns and counties, all containing historical sites and artifacts from the bygone city. Travel the trail through the towns of Calhoun, Port Lavaca, Victoria, Cuero-Meyersville, Yorktown-Hochheim-Yaakum, Gonzales-Smiley, and Seguin, where you can see interesting Indianola artifacts and enjoy the history the towns offer.

BEST TIME TO VISIT

The marker, while moved several times, is still there to see at any season.

Adventures in Lodging and Dining

A wide variety of lodgings is available on the Gulf Coast and along the trail to New Braunfels. As you go down the trail, stop at The BlissWood Bed and Breakfast in Cat Spring, Texas, with its smoke-free environment. Enjoy the turn-of-the-century homes, complete with antiques, settled on over 650 acres of working ranches. Or you might want to stop at the historic Farris Hotel in Eagle Lake. This turn-of-the-century hotel with its antique décor has been refurbished and includes a scenic veranda.

Eating establishments along the trail accommodate a variety of budgets. After a day of antiquing in Cat Spring, Bellville, or Sealy, stop off at Carol's at Cat Spring and enjoy a fine dinner relaxing at a white cloth-covered table either indoors or out on their covered patio. Enjoy the fresh flowers, antiques, and oil paintings while you sip a glass of fine wine from their extensive wine collection.

For More Information

For more on the Indianola Trail, check out the Texas Independence Trail at www.texasindependencetrail.org.

The Seven Museums of the La Salle Odyssey

——— Texas Gulf Coast ———

If you're the type who likes to totally immerse yourself in a story, the ill-fated journey of La Salle is for you. French explorer René-Robert Cavelier Sieur de La Salle dreamed of finding the Mississippi. His search led him across six Texas counties. In a wonderful spirit of cooperation and storytelling, seven Texas Gulf Coast museums have recreated La Salle's Odyssey with each organization or museum focusing on a different part of the story.

When not at home, *La Petite Belle*, a half-scale replica of La Salle's ship, brings the story of the explorer's foray into Texas to every port upon which she calls. Her portable interpretive panels encourage visitors to travel to the Gulf Coast region and learn about this Texas story. Although the building housing the Texas Historical Commission Shipwreck Project in 1996 has since been torn down, the memories of that year will not soon disappear, thanks to the Palacios Area Historical Association. *La Belle*, the ship belonging to La Salle, sunk in 1686 and was excavated from September 1996 to April 1997. All of the artifacts, as well as the hull of the ship, were brought into the headquarters in Palacios before being taken to Texas A&M University for conservation. For further information, visit the website at www.palacioschamber.com/tourist.htm.

ADVENTURES IN HISTORY

In August 1684, René-Robert Cavelier Sieur de La Salle, attempting to find the Mississippi River, crossed the Atlantic with a fleet of four small ships. From the start, tragedy befell the expedition. First Spanish pirates captured one ship. Then, on January 1, 1685, they finally made landfall on the Texas Gulf Coast, only to discover that poor navigation combined with incorrect maps had led the other three ships to an area hundreds of miles from their destination. After they finally arrived, one ship ran aground, and many vital supplies the colonists needed to survive were lost. La Salle's dream had become a nightmare. One of the ships sailed back to France with those who had lost faith in their leader.

About 180 men, women, and children remained with La Salle. He now continued the search for his dream river on the ship *La Belle*, while others stayed behind. The remaining colonists interacted with natives, then tried to establish a colony on Garcitas Creek—Fort St. Louis, the first European colony in Texas. Unfortunately, this did not sit well with the Spanish who claimed the territory. They sent an expedition to destroy the colony, but they were too late. By the time the Spaniards arrived, all the fort's colonists had succumbed to disease and hostile natives. The Spanish buried the French cannons and burned the fort.

In the meantime, early in 1686, *La Belle* hit rough seas and went down beneath the waters of Matagorda Bay. Finally, his own men had enough of La Salle's follies, and they murdered him near present-day Navasota, Texas. La Salle and his disastrous expedition would have remained a misty footnote in history except for a curious diver. More than 300 years later, in 1995, this diver from the Texas Historical Commission discovered a bronze cannon bearing the royal cartouche of France. This led to the discovery of the remains of *La Belle* and drew worldwide attention. Today, thanks to the support from Texans and volunteers from all over the world, the Texas Historical Commission has recovered the oldest French shipwreck in the Western Hemisphere. Texans and visitors alike can share this chapter in Texas state history.

On the Map

The trail of the La Salle Odyssey is primarily in the Texas Gulf Coast area and leads to the various "seven sisters" museums found in Port Lavaca, Corpus Christi, Victoria, Bay City, Edna, Rockport, and Palacios.

Weekend Adventures

• The Calhoun County Museum in Port Lavaca shares the story of French colonial Texas. Artifacts recovered from *La Belle* enhance the insights into the cultural relations between the French and the region's native peoples. Find out how the natives were caught between the Spanish interests and the French colonization attempt. Contact information: phone 361-553-4689.

• The Corpus Christi Museum of Science and History presents both the beginning and the end of the La Salle story. It begins with what La Salle found when he first came to Texas and the impact of the early European settlement on the land and its people. For those who like exhibits, this museum provides many that interpret the science behind the recovery of *La Belle*, and the preservation of the hull and artifacts. Contact information: phone 361-883-2862 (www.ccmuseum.com).

- The Museum of the Coastal Bend, located in Victoria, Texas, presents the story of the first French settlement on Texas soil. A diorama captures the discovery of the eight buried cannons that were unearthed in 1996. Wander through the museum to see artifacts and panels that tell of the uncovering of this long lost settlement. Contact information: phone 361-528-2511 (www.museumofthecoastal bend.org).

- The Matagorda County Museum in Bay City puts the focus on an exhibit of the wreck of *La Belle* with a life-scale diorama of a portion of the ship showing it under excavation. Learn of the events that led up to *La Belle*'s recovery and the last devastating adventure of La Salle's life. Discover how the ship came to rest in Texas and the efforts to save this priceless cultural treasure. Contact information: phone 979-245-1502.

- *La Petite Belle*'s home port is in Palacios, on Matagorda Bay. The half-scale ship is designed along the lines of the original and is a fully functional seagoing vessel. Palacios played host to the excavation during the recovery and gave a great deal of volunteer support to the Texas Historical Commission endeavor.

- The Texana Museum in Edna explores the culture of the Karankawa peoples who lived in the area when La Salle and his colonists arrived. See a life-size diorama of a Karankawa home, interpretive panels and selected artifacts, and discover how contact with Europeans radically altered native Texan life. Contact information: phone 361-782-5431.

- The Texas Maritime Museum in Rockport allows visitors to see the crew of *La Belle* come to life. Explore the museum and learn about the experience of the ship's sailors. There is even a facial reconstruction, based on the skull of one of *La Belle*'s crewmen. While there, view interpretive panels interspersed with artifacts that explain the trade of sailing in the age of exploration. See the art, mystery, and science of navigation. The centerpiece of the exhibit is a 1:12 scale model of *La Belle*. Contact information: phone 361-729-1271 (www.texasmaritimemuseum.org).

BEST TIME TO VISIT

The museums are open year-round, although you might want to plan your trip in conjunction with any annual festivals offered during the year in the various towns.

ADVENTURES IN LODGING AND DINING

Most of the towns will have at least the common chain-type motels found throughout the nation; however, lodging at many historical bed and breakfasts can also be found at the major cities in the Gulf Coast such as Galveston and Houston, or any of the other spots mentioned in the Gulf Coast section. Victoria has an interesting history and plenty to offer, also.

A variety of restaurants is available along the La Salle Odyssey trail.

FOR MORE INFORMATION

Contact the Texas Settlement Region in Victoria, Texas at, 361-485-1570 to learn more and to find out about any current exhibits.

THE SAN ANTONIO MISSION TRAIL

——— SAN ANTONIO, TEXAS ———

Built from 1659 to 1795, Spanish missions dot the Texas landscape. The highest concentration seems to have been in the San Antonio area and is considered to be the highest concentration in North America, as well. Today the San Antonio missions are contained within the San Antonio Missions National Historic Park (www.nps.gov/saan/) and have an annual attendance that is well over one million.

Originally the missions were built in East Texas but later relocated to San Antonio. They served the community in a variety of ways and provided an anchor during a time of constant unrest. Today several of the missions still operate and continue their service to the community and provide the same safe anchor to the locals and to visitors. For many, the park is a historical mecca.

THE MISSIONS OF SAN ANTONIO

- The Alamo—The first mission, the Alamo, is the one with the highest visibility. Alamo Plaza marks the infamous spot where the now world-famous Texas defenders met their fate in their final fight against Santa Anna. With a steady stream of visitors, the chapel is one of the most photographed façades in the nation.
- Mission San José Amphitheatre and Visitors' Center—The San José is the most garrison-like mission and considered to be the largest and best known of the Texas missions.
- Mission Concepción—This is the most beautiful, and the church looks much as it did two hundred years ago.
- Mission San Francisco de la Espada and Espada Dam and Aqueduct—Located further south along the San Antonio River, the mission was formerly called San Francisco de los Tejas. The dam and aqueduct still work, and the mission's working farm is also within the park.
- Mission San Juan Capistrano—The mission has an open bell tower, and the church is still in use.

Currently, the Mission Trails project is still under construction. In addition to the roadways connecting the missions, part of the trail project is open and parallels the San Antonio River. The actual trail will follow nine miles along the San Antonio River. If you're looking for something that combines beauty, history, and charm, then a tour of the San Antonio missions will answer your needs.

ON THE MAP

From downtown San Antonio, go south on St. Mary's Street, which then turns into Roosevelt Avenue and continue south until you reach 3300

Roosevelt. At the intersection of Roosevelt and New Napier Avenue, turn left. The park visitor center will be on the left.

Be Sure to See . . .

The San Antonio Missions Historic Park is an urban park, so roadways connect the various missions. While San Antonio has many historic locations to visit, the Riverwalk Historic District is probably the closest to the missions. The mission park has the San Juan Nature Trail, as well as historical sites and picnic areas along the San Antonio River. Future plans include a hike and bike trail. Campers can call the park to check on possible accommodations. Finished with the missions and San Antonio? There are plenty of small towns to check out such as Converse, Atascosa, and Universal City all within thirty minutes driving distance.

Best Time to Visit

Any time will work, but the park does have an annual Los Pastores event in December and special activities for the Day of the Dead, "Dia de los Muertos," in October. For many, traveling to San Antonio is best when the wildflowers are in bloom during early spring.

Adventures in Lodging and Dining

Two blocks from the park, peacocks and Chinese pheasants roam the grounds of the Marriott Plaza San Antonio. The Havana Riverwalk Inn is quiet and also close to the mission park. But if you want to get real close to the Alamo, the historic Emily Morgan Hotel is next door. For a real San Antonio experience, be sure to walk along the Riverwalk and take in one of the many restaurants.

For More Information

Contact the San Antonio Missions National Park (www.nps.gov/saan/) or the San Antonio Convention Bureau and Visitors Center (www.san antoniocvb.com) or www.sanantoniomissions.areaparks.com.

THE PRESIDENTIAL LIBRARY TRAIL

Presidential stock is rising in Texas. Currently the state is the only state with not one, but two presidential libraries: Austin's Lyndon B. Johnson Library and Museum and College Station's George H. W. Bush Library and Museum. Home of three presidents, Johnson and the Bush father and son, Texas also scores points as having been the birthplace of a fourth president, Dwight D. Eisenhower. Now, with President George W. Bush, the prospects for a third presidential library in Texas are promising. The only question is: Where will it be located?

ADVENTURES IN HISTORY

They've been called shrines, even extravagant mausoleums, but to the National Archives and Records Administration charged with their care, presidential libraries are nothing if they are not time capsules. To those concerned with history and education, the libraries are considered to be some of the most important research sites in America.

But the United States didn't always have specific libraries dedicated to the housing and upkeep of presidential papers and memorabilia. In fact, there are only ten in existence. In 1939 Franklin D. Roosevelt donated his personal and presidential papers to the federal government and spurred the development of the presidential library system.

According to a Knight Ridder article in 2002, the Texas colleges have been scrambling to catch what very well may be the most prized presidential library yet: the George W. Bush Library and Museum. With the possibility of the first father-son library of its type, Texas A&M is eager for the prize. Meanwhile, other colleges stress their ties to Laura Bush, their nearness to the Bush Ranch, or their claim to the president's roots deep in West Texas. In the midst of all this, along came George W.'s former baseball team, the Texas Rangers, offering the land—more than one hundred acres—surrounding Ameriquest Field in Arlington. Whoever wins must have deep financial pockets, but the potential boon to the local economy is enormous.

Meanwhile, Texans and visitors to the state will have to make do with the two presidential libraries currently in full operation. Located at each end of what is called the Presidential Corridor from Austin to College Station, the libraries are busy places with exhibits, forums, and education and research departments. On any given day something is going on. Plan to spend some time when you go.

> Lyndon Baines Johnson Library and Museum
> 2313 Red River Street, Austin, Texas
> www.lbjlib.utexas.edu

I hope that visitors who come here will achieve a closer understanding of the Presidency and that young people will get a clearer comprehension of what this nation tried to do in an eventful period of history.

—Lyndon B. Johnson

Lyndon Baines Johnson's words could be etched above the doorway of every presidential library in the country.

With forty million documents, there is plenty for every visiting scholar to sort through. The museum provides year-round permanent and temporary exhibits. Items on display include the 1968 stretch Lincoln automobile used in Washington and Austin and a mint condition 1910 Model T given to President Johnson by Henry Ford. The car is similar to one LBJ's family had in his youth. In the First Lady's Gallery, visitors will find special personal details of Lady Bird Johnson and her life with the president, including their early love letters and audio-visual clips of life in the White House.

President Johnson was a larger-than-life man, and it takes a larger-than-life library to document his impact on American life.

George Bush Presidential Library and Museum
1000 George Bush Drive, College Station, Texas
http://bushlibrary.tamu.edu

Let future generations understand the burden and blessings of freedom. Let them say we stood where duty required us to stand.

—*George Herbert Walker Bush*

"The Day the Wall Came Down" sculpture by Veryl Goodnight at the George Bush Presidential Library. Vikk Simmons

George Herbert Walker Bush's words still carry weight in today's world. Despite a life dedicated to public service that resulted in an ambassadorship, a vice presidency, and finally the presidency, George H. W. Bush's library is, at its core, intimate and friendly. Like President and Mrs. Bush, the presidential library maintains a family focus despite its vast resources as a presidential archive and museum, and a research institution that is fully integrated into Texas A&M University's academic environment. Events might include the Bush Museum Storytellers Guild presenting original stories and illustrations by "The Family Poet," Wayne Edwards.

Named the number one tourist attraction in East Texas two years in a row by the East Texas Tourism Association, the George Bush Presidential Library and Museum has a lot to offer visitors. More than 38,000,000 pages of personal, vice presidential, and presidential papers lure scholars each and every year. Two million photographs, five thousand videotapes, seven thousand volumes of printed material, and seventy thousand artifacts make up this exceptional resource facility. A large slab of the Berlin Wall greets visitors as they come to the building's entrance. Inside are replicas of Bush's Camp David and Air Force One offices. They offer a glimpse into the real life of a president. Artifacts include a World War II Avenger torpedo bomber and a 1947 Studebaker. The Bush library is the first presidential library to have a classroom that can be used by student groups.

ON THE MAP

The LBJ Presidential Library and Museum sits on the University of Texas campus in Austin, a few blocks north of the Frank Erwin Center. In College Station, the George Bush Presidential Library and Museum is located on a ninety-acre site on the West Campus of Texas A&M University in College Station, the Library and Museum is situated on a plaza adjoining the Presidential Conference Center and the Texas A&M Academic Center.

Weekend Adventures

Lyndon Johnson had a personality as big and sprawling as his LBJ Ranch in the Hill Country. Nearby there is an interpretive center, a living history farm, and the schools LBJ attended. A drive to Fredericksburg is in order to visit the George Bush wing of the new National Museum of the Pacific War. The Commemorative Air Force in Midland, located at the Midland Airport, has an exhibit that is a tribute to President George H. W. Bush, while President George W. Bush's ranch is in Crawford, Texas. A side trip up to Denison puts you in the place where President Dwight D. Eisenhower was born. Visitors to the Eisenhower Birthplace Historical Park can see the two-story frame house and take an Ike Hike through the grounds. The fifth president connected to Texas is President John F. Kennedy. Unfortunately the site Texans can view is not a happy one. The Sixth Floor Museum at Dealey Plaza in Dallas contains items connected to the tragic day when President Kennedy was assassinated.

Best Time to Visit

Ongoing permanent and visiting exhibits are year-round at both presidential libraries. In June, the Bush Library and Museum celebrates the birthdays of President George Herbert Walker Bush, June 12, and Mrs. Barbara Bush, June 8. Call for the exact date of the event. A trip to the Lady Bird Johnson Wildflower Center is in order, especially if you travel to Austin in the spring when the wildflowers and the bluebonnets blanket Texas. After viewing all the LBJ-dedicated institutions, taking a walk through the Wildflower Center is refreshing and renewing.

Adventures in Lodging and Dining

Austin has more than its share of bed and breakfasts, historical hotels, and accommodations for any budget. The College Station/Bryan area also has a range of hotels from the Hilton to chain motels. The La Salle Hotel in Bryan is a Registered Historic Landmark. For a romantic evening, try Bryan's Messina Hof Winery and Resort.

Barn on the Lyndon B. Johnson Historic Park and Historic Site. Vikk Simmons

Dining is never difficult in Austin. A trip to 6th Street is guaranteed to energize and provide plenty of hot spots and restaurants. Christopher's World Grille in Bryan is a 100-year old Texas Ranch home that offers dinner and live jazz on the weekends. Martin's Place, a barbecue restaurant opened in 1925, instantly became a roadhouse/stopping place between Bryan and College Station and recently qualified for a Texas historical marker.

FOR MORE INFORMATION

Contact the Austin Convention and Visitors Bureau (www.austin texas.org) for festivals, fairs, events, restaurants, and hotels. The Bryan/College Station Convention and Visitors Bureau (www.bryan-collegestation.org) has many suggestions for the curious traveler.

2

In and Around Austin

Once a quaint college town, Austin has entered the twenty-first century. Where once the city moved at a steady, slow pace, now Austin moves to the modern rush hour, helter-skelter beat.

No matter how big or how sprawling, Austin will always have a college-town aura. But the town, sometimes called the playground of Texas, is also for outdoor-lovers and nature explorers. Think bats in Texas, and Congress Avenue Bridge comes to mind where 1.2 million bats live during the months of April through October. Nature-lovers the world over seek out the twilight flight of the bats as they come out in the evening to begin their day.

From the beginning, the beauty of Austin's landscape called to visitors. The first glimpse of what was to become the capital of the Lone Star State came during a buffalo-hunting trip in 1838, when the sight of the lush rolling hills reminded Republic of Texas Vice-President Mirabeau B. Lamar of the seven hills that formed the foundation of Rome. His thoughts turned to the new republic, and he knew this area should become the seat of the government. Within months, Lamar succeeded Sam Houston as president and promptly moved the capital from Houston to the hills of Austin.

That same year, 1839, the first steps toward a world-class university began when the Congress of the Republic designated forty acres for the future university. Construction on the first building didn't begin until 1882. As the university expanded, so did the city. No one can deny the impact of the University of Texas on the growth and the culture of the town.

Austin remains the state capital of Texas, and the city is alive with history in the making. Visitors tour the state capital and admire the pink granite domed state capitol building, the capitol complex, and the Texas Governor's mansion. The Austin History Center documents the goings-on of Austin and Travis County, and the Lorenzo de Zavala building of the Texas State Library and Archives contains a genealogical collection. The LBJ Library and Museum attracts visitors from all over the world. After a full day of research or sightseeing, visitors can find a welcome respite at the Sholz Garten, Texas's oldest German "biergarten," where talk can go in many directions, from politics to history, bats to buffaloes.

Today the beat never stops. The sounds of the blues, country, rock and roll, and jazz echo through the Warehouse District on Sixth Street, commonly known as Austin's Music Alley, making Austin the live music capital of the world.

ADVENTURES IN HISTORY

From a trading post in 1838 to the sprawling city of more than a million, Austin has been at the center of Texas history. The state is known for its larger-than-life politicians. Bob Bullock, lieutenant governor of Texas from 1991 to 1999 and one of the most celebrated politicians in recent times, loved history, particularly Texas history. Like most Texans, he dreamed big dreams. The world would send its travelers and history buffs streaming into the capital to visit a grand museum that would be as big as the state it would honor.

An adept politician, Bullock shepherded his dream into reality with a vote by the 1997 Texas Legislature to dedicate $80 million to the museum project. Although Bullock died in 1999, his vision continues. Named for its benefactor, the Bob Bullock Texas State History Museum opened in 2001. A 10-ton, 33-foot bronze Lone Star stands in front in the plaza. "THE STORY OF TEXAS" is carved into the building below the copper dome and announces, in grand terms for all to see, the museum's mission.

The subject is vast: everything you ever wanted to know about the great, big state of Texas. The museum meets the challenge with a variety of maps, exhibitions, timelines and video walls, and interactive stations, all designed to deliver the history of the state in story form. If you shy away from museums because you think they are dry, dark, and stuffy, this new complex will change your mind. Multimedia presentations, mini-theaters, an IMAX theater, and artifacts on loan from museums around the state combine to produce a rich and stimulating experience. If you want to know about Texas history and need a place to start, a trip to the Bob Bullock Texas State History Museum should be at the top of your list.

ON THE MAP

Austin is located in central Travis County on the Colorado River and Interstate 35. The Bob Bullock Texas State History Museum sits on the corner of Congress Avenue and Martin Luther King Boulevard.

WEEKEND ADVENTURES

Austin offers an unusual tour experience with the Austin Duck Tours. After the historic and scenic sites, the tour ends with a cruise in Lake Austin's waters. East Sixth Street or Old Pecan Street was once one of the city's main streets. Now restaurants, shops, clubs, and galleries have given the historical area a rebirth. The Elisabet Ney Museum is a National Historic Site and studio of the famous German sculptress who made Austin and Hempstead her home. For a black history and cultural experience, a trip to the George Washington Carver Museum is in order. The Governor's Mansion, a white-columned mansion built in 1856, draws visitors from the world over and offers public tours Monday through Thursday.

The Lyndon B. Johnson Library and Museum, and the Lady Bird Johnson Wildflower Center, attracts those who love gardening and nature, as well as history. The Neil-Cochran House is the domicile of the National Society of Colonial Dames of America in Texas. Built in 1853, the home features antique furnishings and historical documents. The O. Henry Home, St. Mary's Cathedral, the Texas Military Forces Museum, and the Texas State Cemetery offer more glimpses into Austin and the state's history. A number of walking tours with guides are offered beginning at the steps of the State Capitol, Thursday through Saturday at 9:00 A.M. and Sundays at 2:00 P.M.

BEST TIME TO VISIT

Certainly wildflower-time in the spring is a wonderful time to visit the city and the surrounding Texas Hill Country. For cowboy fans, the Star of Texas Fair and Rodeo in March is a favorite. For an adventurous trip back in time, try the Texas Hill Country Railfair & Festival. Trains include the Austin Steam Train, the Southern Pacific 786 with a 1916 steam engine, and a 1960 diesel locomotive. Music lovers congregate at the Austin City Limits Music Festival in September, while book lovers swarm over the state capital during November's famous Texas Book Festival.

ADVENTURES IN LODGING AND DINING

To experience a bit of famed Texas history, go downtown to the Driskell Hotel on Sixth Street. Built in 1886, the hotel has been called the most celebrated luxury hotel in Texas. This historic and cultural treasure, full of myth, plain old storytelling, and legend, offers a slightly different kind of walking tour. If you enjoy staying overnight in historical districts, try Hyde Park's Woodburn House Bed and Breakfast. The historic Mansion at Judges' Hill has been featured in *Texas Monthly* and has garnered many awards. Austin's Governors' Inn repeatedly receives the *Austin Chronicle*'s "Best B&B in Austin, Texas" award and has been featured on the Travel Channel's Romantic Inns of America.

Whatever your hunger pangs cry out for, Austin is sure to have. The Lodge at Lakeview provides good food coupled with a great view of Lake Austin. Iron Works Barbeque, rated the number one barbeque in Texas, not only offers fine foods but is also set in a former ornamental iron works shop. For the fearless food gourmet, try Hudson's on the Bend, where the chef prepares rabbit, antelope, armadillo, and even rattlesnake dishes.

FOR MORE INFORMATION

The Austin Convention and Visitor Bureau (www.austintexas.org) is located on Sixth Street. The convention bureau maintains a Wildflower Watch (1-800-452-9292) for travelers to let them know when the adjacent Texas Hill Country is in bloom.

O. HENRY'S GIFT TO TEXAS

——— AUSTIN, TEXAS ———

Texas is no stranger to the literary scene, and Austin is a literary town inhabited by a multitude of book lovers. President Lyndon B. Johnson presented James Frank Dobie with the Medal of Freedom for his work. World-renowned novelist James Michener came to know Texas intimately during the writing of his novel *Texas* and in ensuing years donated more than $37 million in gifts to Austin's University of Texas. Austin's Bookpeople is the largest bookstore in Texas, and the Writers League of Texas, formerly Austin's Writers League, maintains a membership of more than 1,200 nationwide. The city has been home to a great many writers at one time or another.

Best known for his short story "Gift of the Magi," O. Henry is an internationally known writer of short stories and one of Austin's favorite literary sons. Born William Sidney Porter, and raised in Greensboro, North Carolina, Porter is generally considered to be a New York author, and few associate him with Texas. However, he spent the years from 1882 to 1897 in the great state and set forty-two of his stories in Texas.

In fact, you could argue that the world's view of Texas and Texans could be laid at his feet. During his time in Texas, he tended sheep, worked ranches, and listened to the tales of cowhands. He drew on his friendship with Lee Hall, a Texas Ranger and ranch foreman, and used him as a model in a couple of stories. With stories full of sketches about life in Texas, an illustrated history of Indian battles entitled *Indian Depredations in Texas*, and his own weekly tabloid, the *Rolling Stone*, Porter brought his vision of Texas to life in the minds of millions.

Today the O. Henry Museum, located in downtown Austin, is the home where Porter and his wife lived from 1893–1895. He spent much of his time downtown, and visitors can still follow in his footsteps and walk past the same buildings that had such an impact on his life, including the Old Federal Courthouse, the Bismark Saloon, old Millett Opera House, and the Texas General Land Office Building. Unfortunately, Porter's life in Austin and his romance with Texas changed dramatically during his tenure at the First National Bank in Austin.

Adventures in History

Texans are not strangers to banking scandals, and William Sidney Porter's certainly numbers among them. For many years Porter lived what many would call an adventurous and romantic life, but his luck turned when he accepted a job at the First National Bank in Austin. Accused of embezzlement in 1894, Porter resigned and devoted his time to his newspaper, the *Rolling Stone*. When the newspaper folded, he moved to Houston to write a column for the *Houston Post*.

In 1896 federal bank examiners charged him with embezzlement. After he was arrested on Valentine's Day, his father bailed him out of jail. With a trial in the works for the summer, Porter must have gotten cold feet, because he left Austin and caught a steamer for Honduras. Maybe he thought he could wait out the statute of limitations and return later.

Whatever his reasons for running away, Porter soon faced a family crisis that forced him to return. His beloved wife, who had fought a long battle with tuberculosis, suffered a severe decline. Being so far from his wife proved to be more than Porter could endure, and he returned to Austin to care for her. She died July 25, 1897. Seven months later, Porter was convicted of embezzlement and received a five-year sentence.

The state sent Porter to a penitentiary in Columbus, Ohio, to serve out his sentence. In her book, *Time to Write: How William Sidney Porter Became O. Henry*, co-author Jenny Lind Porter-Scott, says Porter considered suicide when he first went to jail. Over time he turned to writing, and Porter-Scott says prison actually gave him the time to do some serious writing. In prison he adopted the name O. Henry.

He never returned to Texas. After an early release, he moved to New York where he died with only a few pennies in his pocket. His conviction continues to be controversial. Although Porter denied the charges, he never did much in the way of a defense, and the mystery remains to this day. There are those who believe two of his stories hold clues to the mystery of his bank dealings that ultimately led to the embezzlement charges.

Today O. Henry's memory and his writings are remembered during the annual birthday bash held every September.

ON THE MAP

The museum is located in downtown Austin at 409 East 5th Street.

WEEKEND ADVENTURES

Many of O. Henry's materials can be found in the Austin History Center, part of the Austin Public Library. Collections can be found in the Harry Ransom Humanities Research Center and the Center for American History. The Visitor's Center of the State Capitol Complex on the second floor has the Draughtsman's Room where Porter worked and visitors can still see the desk he used. For some insight into Porter's romantic soul, stop by the home of Dr. R. K. Smoot and see the windowsill where Porter scratched his wife's name one night when they dated. The good doctor also performed the wedding ceremony when Porter married Athol Estes. The O. Henry Hall, once used as a courthouse, is part of the University of Texas campus. The university's walking tour includes a number of museums such as the Texas Memorial Museum, with its collection of antique firearms, and the LBJ Library and Museum with its replica of the Oval Office. Don't miss a visit to the Harry Ransom Center for a view of the center's rare Gutenberg Bible.

Best Time to Visit

There are two annual O. Henry attractions. The O. Henry Pun-Off World Championships, held at the O. Henry Museum on the first Sunday of May, draws participants from across the nation. The O. Henry Birthday Celebration, which takes place on the Sunday closest to September 11, celebrates Porter's birthday. The annual Texas Book Festival, inspired by former First Lady of Texas Laura Bush, is held in November.

Adventures in Lodging and Dining

A member of the Historic and Hospitality Accommodations of Texas, the Governor's Inn bed and breakfast is the recipient of numerous awards and has been featured on the Travel Channel's Romantic Inns of America. All ten rooms are named for Texas governors.

For a restaurant with style and history, try the historic Paggi House. Located at Lamar and Lee Barton Drive, the building housing the restaurant became something of a cause for historic preservationists, the site for an archeological dig, and finally became listed in the National Register. The old stone buildings that now contain the offices and bathrooms were once a milk room and servant's quarters.

For More Information

The Austin Parks and Recreation Department maintains the O. Henry Museum.

Brenham Adopts a Texas Hero

Brenham, Texas

Anyone who has discovered Brenham, Texas, wants to return to the town that can easily be called an open, filled-to-the-brim treasure chest. Although Brenham is the business heart of Washington County, the town is considered to be the birthplace of Texas. Brenham likes to say it offers the perfect escape and encourages its visitors to revive, rejuvenate, and relax.

As a small settlement known as Hickory Grove, the town began on one hundred acres of land donated by Arabella Harrington, who had received a land grant of 4,428 acres from Mexico in 1831. In 1843, the name changed to Brenham, and the next year the town became the seat of Washington County. When the Washington County Railroad made the town a terminus in 1860, Brenham became a major distribution center. Several more railroads added to the town's prosperity. Brenham suffered the burning of commercial buildings during Reconstruction, major fires, and a yellow fever epidemic, yet its population doubled every census. The heavy migration of Germans into the area gave the town the character it still displays. The "Maifest," a May festival, originated from the Germans' "Volksfests."

Brenham entered into the state's Main Street Program in 1983 and began a revitalization of the downtown area. Today the Historic Main Street District offers great shopping—more than forty shops—and has been named a National Register District for three consecutive years.

Adventures in History

Born in Kentucky in 1810, Richard Fox Brenham's parents surely never imagined that their son would not only die a martyr for the Texas Republic but also have a town named after him. Leading an apparently uneventful life, young Brenham attended Transylvania College in Lexington, Kentucky, and became a surgeon before moving to Texas before the revolution. He served three months in the Texas army in 1836 and received a 320-acre tract in Cooke County, although no one knows whether he ever really took possession of the land.

For the next five years, Brenham practiced medicine part-time in Austin. In 1841, President Lamar chose Dr. Brenham for one of the civil commissioners of the Texan Santa Fe Expedition that was charged with the mission of gathering the city of Santa Fe and part of the trade along the Santa Fe Trail under the new Republic's control.

The mission failed.

The Mexican authorities arrested the various group members of the Santa Fe Pioneers during September and October 1841 and transported them to Mexico City. Released in 1842, the doctor returned to Austin, only to join the Somervell expedition against Mexico. This expedition proved successful and resulted in the capture of Laredo, Texas, and Guerrero, Tamaulipas. Afterwards, the volunteers were ordered to disband; however, Brenham and others were not ready to return home. Instead, they decided to join the ill-fated Mier expedition. On the way from Matamoros to Mexico City, Brenham took part in the fighting and died. Richard Fox Brenham died a hero on February 11, 1843.

Within a year, the Hickory Grove community changed its name to Brenham to honor the doctor who had served them so well.

ON THE MAP

Brenham is at the intersection of U.S. 290 and Texas 105, 68 miles west of Houston, 88 miles east of Austin, and 40 miles south of Bryan-College Station.

WEEKEND ADVENTURES

Opportunities for a walk into the past occur around every corner in Brenham. The 1869 Giddings-Stone Mansion has been ranked as one of the ten best examples of nineteenth-century residential architecture in Texas. Visit the Brenham Heritage Museum and immediately see the 1879 Silsby Steam Fire Engine, bought for $3,000. A stroll through Fireman's Park reaps major rewards, but be sure to make arrangements ahead of time if you want to see the 1912 C.W. Parker carousel. Henderson Park, established in 1920 to serve the black community, is one of Brenham's oldest parks. The Brenham Heritage Museum, housed in Brenham's circa 1915 Post Office, is listed on the National Register of Historic Places.

A few side trips bring more historical pleasures. Take Highway 390 north and Highway 105 east to Washington-on-the-Brazos, a 293-acre park known as the birthplace of Texas, to find the spot where the Texas leaders met to sign the Texas Declaration of Independence in 1836. This exact replica of Independence Hall, a Washington-on-the-Brazos State Historic Site, is the place where the document so treasured and so fiercely fought for by so many Texans, was signed. Not too far off is the Star of Republic Museum. Before you leave, stop by the Barrington Living History Farm, where a full range of sights, sounds, and smells recreate a southern cotton plantation. For more of the days when "cotton reigned supreme," take a side trip to Burton and see the historic Burton Cotton Gin and Museum. Then it's on to the Chappell Hill Historic District, the Gateway to Washington County. To experience colonial Texas life, stop at the John P. Coles House in Independence.

BEST TIME TO VISIT

Although a visit to Brenham is enjoyable any day of the year, surely the best time is when the bluebonnets are in bloom and the Bluebonnet Trails beckon winter-weary travelers. For a dance around the Maypole and a drink in the "das grosse Bierzelt," big beer tent, many plan their trips to coincide with the annual "Maifest," a tradition dating back to 1874.

ADVENTURES IN LODGING AND DINING

Many tourists stay in Brenham but travel the hillsides antiquing in Navasota, Bellville, and Round Top. Others take in the history at Independence, Chappell Hill, and Washington-on-the-Brazos State Historical

Park. The town has been referred to as a Bed and Breakfast bonanza. The Ant Street Inn is a former Super Savitall, meat market, and deli, that has been renovated into a charming bed and breakfast with high-ceilinged bedrooms, even a ballroom. Ask about Room 209—the room with the freight elevator in the center. The Schuerenberg House, a restored Victorian mansion, is a recorded Texas Historic Landmark and is listed in the National Register of Historic Places.

A trip to Brenham is incomplete without a visit to the Bluebell Creameries, established in 1907 as the Brenham Creamery Company. The Must Be Heaven and Fluff Top Roll Restaurants are two well-known eateries. For a dash of history with your meal, stop by the Citizens Pharmacy, complete with early pharmaceutical artifacts and its soda fountain and grill.

For More Information

Contact the Brenham website at www.brenhamtexas.com for the Visitor's Guide with maps for Brenham, Burton, Chappell Hill, Independence, and Washington. The Washington County Chamber of Commerce provides free maps of the Bluebonnet Trails. Check its website for the online Wildflower Watch to get the latest in bluebonnet updates on the best places to view the blue-carpeted countryside and for an updated calendar of events.

Polka, Kolaches, and Train Wrecks

West, Texas

Let's dance! That seems to be the cry throughout the town of West, Texas. However, this wasn't always case. In the 1840s people settled in West, Texas, to farm the rich lands and raise cattle. The farmers grew cotton, maize, and wheat in an area centered around Bold Springs, a fresh water spring. In 1881, the Katy Railroad cut a swath through property owned by Thomas W. West, and a new train depot was built on the land West sold to the railroad. More land was sold to folks wanting to open businesses along the tracks. West then served as postmaster in the new post office opened beside the depot. He also ran a general store and later engaged in several other businesses as well. In 1892, West, Texas, the center of area commerce, became a town named in honor of this successful businessman.

Business boomed with the advent of the railroad, and before long many Czechs arrived to take advantage of the fertile soil and to start businesses of their own. With them came the custom of having large families, and they soon became the dominant culture in West. Another of their customs was a love of music and dance, particularly the polka. Many of the people living in West today are direct descendents of the Czechoslovakians who came to West all those years ago. When you come to town, you might even hear some of the older folks speaking the Czechoslovakian language. The town of West is well known for its restaurants and bakeries specializing in Czech and German foods. West prides itself as the Czech Heritage Capital of Texas, and home of the official kolache of the Texas Legislature. The historical Nemecek Brothers Meat Market, established in the late 1800s, is famous throughout Texas for its Czech hams and sausages.

Besides garnering fame for its unusual foods, thanks to the ambition of a passenger agent for the Katy Railroad, West also has a fascinating legend to add to its history. You can't talk about railroads and trains without the story of the town that lived for a day, Crush, Texas. This spectacular event took place just 3 miles outside of West. For one entire day in 1886, Crush, Texas, was the second largest city in the state. By midnight the city no longer existed.

ADVENTURES IN HISTORY

Generating favorable publicity was the main idea behind the creation of the ill-fated town of Crush, Texas. Located on the Texas prairie near Waco, the bizarre event brought out over 40,000 spectators. The idea behind this stunt belonged to William George Crush, a passenger agent for the Missouri, Kansas, and Texas Railroad, also known as the Katy Railroad. What if, he conjectured, two locomotives crashed head-on causing an enormous collision? His excitement over the gigantic crash must have been contagious since he easily convinced the Katy Railroad officials that it would be a great way to promote the railroad, thereby generating a good deal more business.

Concerned about the safety issue, Crush checked with several engineers. All but one assured him the boilers would be fine. Since most were sure, he ignored the one man who claimed that the boilers would burst and kill many people.

Crush had one engine painted bright red and the other bright green, sent out ads, and employed a couple of hundred constables to handle the troublemakers and the pickpockets who were common at that time. The railroad set up tents, supplied water, and built a wooden jail. They even promised the public that the vendors would not gouge them with excessive prices. A crowd of about 20,000 was expected, but the estimated numbers ranged from 40,000 to 50,000. Since the event was free and no tickets were sold, the actual attendance figures remain a mystery.

The action went something like this.

A large crowd gathers on the hillsides under the sweltering Texas sun. Two trains face each other down miles of empty rail. Deputies herd excited onlookers back out of possible harm's way. William Crush signals the start, and people shout as the two metal giants spew steam and smoke while the shrill sound of the train's whistles cuts the air. With the throttles tied open, the engineers and fireman leap from the engines and rush into the crowd. On the single track, the two locomotives pulling their cars hurtle toward one another.

A gargantuan crash is heard. The two trains smash into each other, rise into the air, and slowly settle to earth. Another deafening roar splits the quiet. The boilers have burst, sending thousands of chunks of metal hurtling down on the crowd. They try to escape, but the swarm of humanity is too much. In the bloody aftermath, one Confederate soldier is heard to say, "It is like a Civil War battle—people falling all around me." As the spectators realize the danger has passed, they push toward the site of the smoking ruins, reaching for souvenirs and burning their fingers on the hot metal. And Crush? He's fired that day.

Ironically, despite the day's horror, the event had accomplished its purpose. The Crash at Crush garnered many headlines around the world, and the Katy Railroad's business picked up. Within a few days, the railroad had rehired Crush. He then spent the next fifty-seven years in service to that railroad. If not for the fact that this stunt ended in tragedy, the sound of locomotives crashing might have been heard all over the country in brand-new cities lasting only a day.

On the Map

The town of West, Texas, is located on Interstate 35 eighty miles south of Dallas in northeastern McLennan County. The marker for Crush is a plaque located about fifteen miles north of Waco in McLennan County and accessible to the public.

Weekend Adventures

For a quick visit to the past, visit the West Depot, home for a railroad museum as well as the information center for West. Along with old photographs of the railroad, you'll also find West's original phone operator's station. Not only photos of the crash at Crush but also actual pieces of the wrecked trains are on display, as well as detailed accounts by spectators to that long-ago ill-fated publicity stunt.

All that remains of the town of Crush is a roadside marker placed at the site of the crash in 1977. Other than that, old newspaper accounts, court records, and a few photographs are the only other things left to see. To hear the song written by Scott Joplin, as well as Joplin's other works, check out Lone Star Junction's Songs of Texas Web page at www.lsjunction.com/midi/songs.htm.

Best Time to Visit

Share the Czechoslovakian cultural history every Labor Day weekend when West invites people from all over to their annual Westfest Gala, a Czech/polka festival celebrating the town's Czechoslovakian heritage.

ADVENTURES IN LODGING AND DINING

For a sense of history, travel a few miles south and stay at the Judge Baylor House in Waco. Named for Judge Baylor, the founder of Baylor University, the award-winning bed and breakfast is only a couple of blocks away from the Armstrong-Browning Library that houses the largest collection of materials related to Elizabeth and Robert Browning.

For old-fashioned goodness, head to Kolacek's Bakery. The family uses old Czech recipes that tempt many to select this bakery for their famous traditional kolaches. Nemecek Bros., located on the same site as its original wooden building in 1896, is the oldest family business in West. Although it is not a restaurant, you're in for some fine dining when you take home any of their fresh meats. While times have changed, the family tradition of excellence has remained the same.

FOR MORE INFORMATION

The West Chamber of Commerce is online at www.westchamber.com.

FORGING A LASTING FRIENDSHIP

——— FREDERICKSBURG, TEXAS ———

Fredericksburg is a town steeped in history. It's in the very air you breathe. Visitors can easily spend days exploring the town's history, rich in German heritage, and, in fact, the nation's. Texans seem to suffer from a huge case of spring flight, with many climbing into their cars and heading for the Hill Country, so it's not unusual for these fevered travelers to suddenly find themselves entering this old bastion of German heritage. With its architectural charm and the lure of hearty German

Old buildings line the streets of downtown Fredericksburg.
Vikk Simmons

food and ale, travelers often lose their need to move on and instead slow down to immerse themselves in the quaint charm of this historical town.

Indianola welcomed more than five thousand German immigrants, and Central Texas played host to most of them. The trip wasn't easy. Not only did these stoic travelers have to deal with sickness and poor or nearly non-existent transportation, but the war between Mexico and the United States played havoc with their journeys. On May 8, 1846, the settlers founded Fredericksburg, and over time the Germans overcame obstacles, negotiated peace with the Indians, and set about establishing a healthy, vital community.

Today Fredericksburg honors all the hard work and sacrifices the early colonists made by retaining much of the Old World charm created by its founders. The town has become a mecca for Hill Country travelers with its Victorian gingerbread-bedecked homes, old-time churches, and a grand courthouse. This peaceful, tourist-oriented town charms the constant stream of travelers who tour the area.

ADVENTURES IN HISTORY

Fredericksburg has its roots in an organization called the Society to Protect German Immigrants in Texas or, as it was known in 1842, the "Adelsverein" or noble's association. Dedicated to making sure all German immigrants had everything they needed to begin a new life, the society bought property for settlement in the Republic of Texas and supplied the immigrants with land, food, houses, wagons, oxen, horses, corn, seed, and even tools. The Germans, who landed in Indianola, loaded their wagons and trundled toward the newly purchased land called New Braunfels. By 1846 New Braunfels had all the immigrants it could handle.

The society had already appointed Commissioner General Baron Ottfried Hans Freiherr von Meusebach. Thirty-two years old, red-haired and blue-eyed, the tall baron knew what he faced and set out to find a new place for settlement. He bought 10,000 acres northwest of New Braunfels on credit and named it Fredericksburg in honor of Prince Friedrich of Prussia. Unfortunately, the land north of the town happened also to be the land of 6,000 Comanche Indians.

The Verein's Fisher-Miller Grant contract had conditions. Peace with the Indians had to be fulfilled by 1847, or the purchase of the land would be in jeopardy. Seven years earlier, thirteen Comanche chieftains lay dead after the fatal San Antonio Council House, and the Indians responded with a bloody raid on the towns of Victoria and Linnville. Meusebach knew he would face the same warriors from the earlier raids. Not an easy task. Not one for the faint-hearted. In the end, Meusebach, called Red Sun or "chief with the burning hair of the head" by the Indians, negotiated the treaty.

Today visitors to the History Walk behind Fredericksburg's Vereinskirche Museum will find the sculpture *Lasting Friendship* that depicts the moment Meusebach received the peace pipe from Comanche Chief Buffalo Hump during the 1847 treaty negotiation.

On the Map

Located about 70 miles northwest of San Antonio and 75 miles west of Austin, Fredericksburg is in the area commonly known as the Texas Hill Country.

Weekend Adventures

Another New Braunfels favorite son, Chester William Nimitz, had a highly successful naval career and served as Fleet Admiral during World War II. Later, his boyhood home, the Nimitz Hotel, became the Admiral Nimitz Museum. Today the museum has evolved into the National Museum of the Pacific War, with 34,000 square feet of indoor exhibit space, displays of Allied and Japanese aircraft, tanks, guns, and many other artifacts. The center is located on nine acres and offers visitors a chance to go back in time and experience Guadalcanal and the epic struggle in the Pacific. The Japanese Garden of Peace, a replica of Admiral Toga's garden, is a gift from the military leaders of Japan to the United States people in honor of Admiral Nimitz.

Fredericksburg has much more to see. The historic district is the heart of the city and makes for a wonderful walking tour with over eighty points of interest. Music lovers will want to stop by Hill Country Dulcimers and watch the making of dulcimers, while Civil War buffs will focus on the Fort Martin Scott Historic Site on East Main, a pre–Civil War military outpost. The Pioneer Museum Complex began with a home, a smokehouse, and a barn and has grown to include six more historical structures. The Vereinkirche Museum has a number of permanent exhibits and photographs.

BEST TIME TO VISIT

Many Texans like to visit the Hill Country and follow the Wildflower Trail during the spring when the wildflowers are in bloom. Concerts and special events, such as the Founders Festival and the Christmas Home Tour, are presented throughout the year, but for a real heart-felt oompah experience plan to visit during the annual Octoberfest. To celebrate the beginning of Fredericksburg, be sure and stop by during the Founders Day Festival in May.

ADVENTURES IN LODGING AND DINING

The Haussegen Log House & Fachwerk Cottage offers visitors a chance to stay in a restored 1770s log home and experience life in an early Texas home. Designed by Edward Stein, the designer of the Gillespie County Courthouse, the Magnolia House is designated by the Texas Historical Commission for The Recorded Texas Historic Landmark. The Alte Welt Gasthof Bed and Breakfast has earned the Historic Accommodations of Texas's Great Stays of Texas award. This Old World inn operates out of a 1915 building. A visit to the Fredericksburg Brewing Company, an 1890s historical building with an inside "biergarten," involves food, beer, and pastries. For a slightly more modern structure, the Hilltop Café serves food in a 1926 filling station.

FOR MORE INFORMATION

The city's official site is www.fbgtx.org, while the Fredericksburg Texas Visitors Bureau is at www.fredericksburg-texas.com. For historical information contact the Gillespie County Historical Society at www.pio neermuseum.com.

Following the Indianola Trail:
The "Come and Take It" City

Gonzales, Texas

The very first skirmish of the Texas Revolution took place in Gonzales, earning the town the nickname "Lexington of Texas." The only town to retain its name from the days of Spanish rule, Gonzales was also the first Anglo-American settlement west of the Colorado River. While Lieutenant Colonel William B. Travis commanded a small band at the Alamo in February of 1836 and tried to frame the constitution of the Republic of Texas, Santa Anna began his siege of the Alamo. Thirty-two volunteers from Gonzales, known as the Immortal 32, answered Travis's call for help—the only town to send reinforcements to the Alamo.

When General Sam Houston arrived in Gonzales, he heard the news of the fall of the Alamo. Fearing Gonzales would be next and refusing to give any aid to the advancing Mexican army, Houston ordered his army of volunteers to burn Gonzales to the ground. When Houston and his men left town, a retreat later known as the Runaway Scrape, they made their first stop at what has become known as the Branches House. Houston and his several hundred citizen-soldiers rested their horses beneath an oak tree, later referred to as the Sam Houston Oak. There, they stood and watched the glow on the horizon as Gonzales burned to the ground. Eventually, Houston's troops defeated the Mexican army at San Jacinto and secured Texas's independence.

Today, the Oak, the house, and the land remain. They became the setting for the book and television series *True Women*.

Adventures in History

With the firing of a single shot, Gonzales propelled the talks with Mexico into what is thought to be the first battle of the Texas Revolution. Mexico had given Gonzales a cannon for protection against the Indians. One day the Mexican authorities decided they wanted their cannon returned. When the first group of five Mexican soldiers arrived with their ox cart, the people of Gonzales sent them on their way minus the cannon. The Mexican government then sent one hundred men to collect what they considered their property. However, the response they received was anything but amicable. Not ready to return their gift, the Texans, under Colonels John H. Moore and J. W. E. Wallace, loaded the cannon with scrap iron and fired. Only one casualty resulted from the ensuing fight.

The Texans waved their battle flag. The Come and Take It flag, as it was known, afforded the battle a great deal of recognition. The flag, white with the image of the old cannon and emblazoned with a star, got its name from the words "come and take it" printed in black below the picture of the cannon. The Mexicans retreated. On this second day of October in 1835, the first shot was fired in the Texas war of independence.

On the Map

Gonzales is located in the north central part of the county where the Guadalupe and San Marcos Rivers come together, and on U.S. Highways 90, 97, and 183.

Weekend Adventures

There are plenty of historical sites to see. The inner town is composed of seven public squares that form a Spanish cross true to the early Mexican and the Roman Catholic traditions. The squares include Confederate Square and Texas Heroes Square. The current seat of Gonzales County, the 1887 Gonzales County Courthouse, listed in the National Register of Historic Places, was restored to the tune of $3 million in 1998. A drive through town will reveal sixty-four historical markers pointing out highlights of the town's architecture. The 1887 Old Jail Museum houses the Chamber of Commerce and once played host to many of the West's wanted men, including John Wesley Hardin.

Visitors might have fun checking the myth about the 1896 courthouse clock and the killer Albert Howard who cursed the clock. Howard was the last man hanged there. Prior to his scheduled hanging, the clock, which had four sides, had always worked just fine. Proclaiming his innocence, Howard cursed the timepiece as he stared at it counting down the hours before his hanging. He swore the clock would never work right again, thereby proving his innocence. When he was hanged, the four clock faces went wild. According to legend, the four clock faces never showed the same time as each other again. Over the years the courthouse clock has been repaired, been damaged—twice by lightning—and repaired again. Some still wonder whether Howard had truly been guilty. Today the clock works.

To take a tour of Gonzales, start at the Old Jail Museum and inspect the historic properties and sites, including the frame homes. Built of cypress wood because it seldom rotted, the frame houses were rarely damaged by termites. The Come and Take It cannon and other artifacts can be found at the Memorial Museum. The Historical Trail is a driving tour with 86 historical points of interest. The First Shot Photo & Carriage offers tours, ranch carriage rides and photo opportunities. A number of restored wagons and carriages are also on display. Finally, a trip north of town to Pioneer Village with its nine restored buildings gives visitors a chance to experience Old Gonzales.

BEST TIME TO VISIT

The last weekend in April is a great time for history buffs since it's the time of the Historic Homes on Tour, offering an historical program and demonstrations, as well as the Gonzales Pioneer Village Living History Center's special events. The annual Come and Take It Celebration held on the first full weekend of October marks the first shot for Texas independence. Included in the events are a parade, music, and a battle reenactment at Pioneer Village.

ADVENTURES IN LODGING AND DINING

For a taste of history, Gonzales offers several fine bed and breakfasts. The Belle Oaks Inn, an inspected and approved member of Historic Accommodations of Texas and known as one of the great stays in Texas, is a completely restored Louisiana-plantation-style house. The St. James Inn Bed and Breakfast, awarded a AAA three-diamond rating, was once the home of Walter Kokernot, the son of David Levi Kokernot, a Texas hero and personal confidant of General Sam Houston. The home is built in transitional period mansion style and filled with nine fireplaces and plenty of antiques. Rumors suggest that Kokernot's ghost roams the halls looking for his daughter.

For steak and seafood try Boudreaux on DeWitt Drive. Looking for lunch? There's Opie's Cow Palace, which serves a wide range of meals, or for home-cooked meals give Café on the Square on St. Joseph Street a try. The Gonzales Food Market offers old-fashioned barbecue and a dining room or take-out—the fun is eating on butcher paper if you choose.

FOR MORE INFORMATION

Contact the Gonzales Local and Tourist Information or the Gonzales Chamber of Commerce and Agriculture at their website at www.gonza lestexas.com.

LEGENDS: FACT AND FICTION

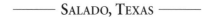

——— SALADO, TEXAS ———

Salado is well known as a great place to shop and as a treasure trove of art and artists, but the town is also steeped in history and imbued with legend. After the financial Panic of 1819, many people sought their futures in the West, and Salado, Texas, was one destination.

Sterling C. Robertson obtained land grants from Mexico and offered the land in the Brazos River Valley to homesteaders. Some thirty counties in Texas were carved from this one land grant, but not many settled in Salado at the time. Old records show only 57 whites settled along the 35-mile stretch of Salado Creek

People came to the Salado area for many reasons. Indian lore held that Salado Creek had special curative powers, and this promise drew some early settlers. As more and more people settled along the creek area, the number of dwellings increased, and residents wanted a town and education opportunities. In 1859, Colonel Robertson donated one hundred acres for a town and a college. Salado remained a small village until the 1960s when revitalization of the town began in earnest.

Salado remains true to its nature as a small historic village but has grown in scope and is well known for its artisans, quaint shops, lodging, and interesting stories.

ADVENTURES IN HISTORY

While Salado had many interesting tales to tell, two stand out from the rest. In 1859 the board of Salado College influenced the legislature to stop the sale of intoxicating beverages. They also proposed keeping what they called billiard saloons and ten pin alleys off any land donated by Sterling C. Robertson for college purposes. A soldier passing through the town in 1869 noted that Salado was certainly a total abstinence village.

But things changed suddenly when the entire county, which included Salado, was declared "WET." Of course, a saloon immediately opened and attracted the attention of the young men in town.

According to a popular tale, the unhappy ladies of Salado were unable to get the owner to close what they decided was his den of iniquity. So the women devised a plan to discourage customers. Two at a time, the ladies took turns sitting in the saloon and knitting. The ladies knew no man or boy would venture into the place as long as they were there. After only one day's vigil, the saloonkeeper closed his doors, and no other similar place has opened in Salado since.

There are many tales of hauntings in the town of Salado. One of the supposed treasure sites was a sizeable cave near the Stagecoach Inn. Originally the cave was a play area with a large tree inside. Kids would

Giant armadillo in Johnson City. Vikk Simmons

climb the tree and swing from its limbs. But through years of use and low maintenance, the cave became littered and overgrown. The owner at that time decided it was no longer safe and closed it to visitors. Because this occurred during the Depression era, he didn't have any money to clear out the cave; however, another townsman had an idea.

He knew people believed the area had treasure and liked to hunt for it. So he asked a lady he knew to send a letter to a wealthy man telling of a cave in Salado rumored to contain gold. It wasn't long before the man appeared. No one knows the exact conversation, but the rich man was given permission to clear out the cave.

There were plenty of young men eager to find work in those days, and the man paid them to remove many buckets of debris from the cave. While nothing was found for days, the man remained optimistic. But, eventually, he lost patience, and the project was abandoned. No one knows if anything of value was ever unearthed, but the cave was now clean, no money had been spent on the project, and it had provided employment. The town thought that was treasure enough. Although the gold was apparently a rumor, the Village of Salado continues to say this story is true.

On the Map

Centrally located, Salado is an easy drive from most areas of Texas. Salado is located on Interstate 35 between Austin and Waco.

Weekend Adventures

Salado is a tourist's paradise with plenty of historical sites and even more shopping opportunities. Many artists make Salado their home, and their art is the treasure lying open for all eyes to see. Take a trip to Salado Creek to see Tablerock, a large limestone monolith that served as a meeting place for local Native Americans and was once a trysting spot for the local college students until a flood in 1921 undermined the rock and caused it to tilt.

Today the Tablerock Festival of Salado and its Goodnight Amphitheater serve as a theatrical venue for many festivals, concerts, programs, and plays throughout the year. In addition, take in the dinner theater, Salado Legends, historic Twelve Oaks, a Greek Revival house, and the old wagon wheel ruts cut into the rock from the Old Chisholm Trail that runs along the creek.

The structures in Baines House residence include the home of George Washington Baines, great grandfather of President Lyndon Baines Johnson. Rose Mansion, the main home built in 1870, contains Texas Markers and a National Register marker, and consists of two beautifully restored log cabins, a summer kitchen cottage, and a larger Greek Revival cottage.

Best Time to Visit

History and charm greet travelers any day of the week. For art-lovers, a trip to Salado in August to attend the annual August Art Fair is a treat. The annual event for more than thirty-seven years includes a display of fine pottery. While there, take a stroll on one of the historic green walking bridges. When the weather is a bit cooler and the countryside a bit more colorful, visit during the spring Wildflower Art Show.

Adventures in Lodging and Dining

There are many fine places to stay in Salado. A year-round favorite, and a great historical experience, is the Stagecoach Inn, named the Best Historic Inn by *Texas Highways* magazine. Once known as the Shady Villa Inn, the inn is located on the Chisholm Trail. The guest book reads like a frontier Who's Who with names of such notables as: General George A. Custer, Robert E. Lee, Sam Houston, and Jesse James. The Rose Mansion, with its early Texas Greek Revival home, cottages, and log cabins is a great place for weary travelers. The Levi Tenney House might be the oldest building in Salado and is listed in the National Register of Historic Places. The Inn at Salado, Salado's first bed and breakfast, is within walking distance to shops and restaurants in town. It displays both a Texas Historical Marker and a National Register listing.

Restaurants abound in Salado and include the Ambrosia Tearoom and The Range at the Baron House, ranked in the top ten restaurants by *Texas Monthly*. The Salado Mansion restaurant is part of early Salado history. Built in 1857, it was owned by the first mayor of Salado and serves a blend of Tex-Mex and southwestern food. A perfect mix for a house that claims to be where Texas history was made.

FOR MORE INFORMATION

Contact the Salado Chamber of Commerce (www.salado.com) or e-mail the Village of Salado (www.villageofsalado.com) with questions.

LOVE IS IN THE AIR

—— WACO, TEXAS ——

Once named Six-Shooter Junction, Waco, Texas, is a town comprised of love and beauty. Known as the home of Texas hospitality, Waco welcomes you with a big smile and plenty of Texas history. In 2001, Heritage Square, a revitalized downtown park, opened to the public. The square invites visitors to wander down the shaded walkways, enjoy the water-play fountain, and experience a unique gathering-place. Visitors can take in restaurants and shops and continue with a river walk along the Brazos River that begins at Ft. Fisher Park, goes past the Texas Ranger Museum, the *Brazos Belle* river boat, and ends at the Waco Suspension Bridge.

While some may not find any beauty in a bridge, not so the pioneers who made up early Waco. Today this engineering feat is the city's centerpiece and unites both sides of the river, but in the early days, the townspeople didn't have any way of taking a wagon across the river. In 1866 a group of bold city leaders envisioned a bridge that would allow for the passage of wagons. They quickly raised the needed $135,000, hired an architect, and approved the work. Construction began in 1869. Nearly three million red bricks covered the 475-foot span to make up the first single-span bridge west of the Mississippi. Most important, Waco now had a way for wagons to cross the Brazos River. This allowed the Texas Chisholm Trail to pass straight through Waco and played an important part in the growth of the West.

"How do I love thee? Let me count the ways," said the poet, and her words have taken on a special meaning for the people of Waco. Baylor University's Armstrong-Browning Library, called the most beautiful building in the world, houses the largest collection of Robert and Elizabeth Barrett Browning's work. Fifty-eight stained-glass windows illuminate passages of the Brownings' poetry, but they are but one part of the sensory arsenal the building projects upon unsuspecting viewers. Visitors whisper the words or silently repeat them in their minds as they make their way through the building, treading across marble floors, gazing at intricate designs on high ceilings, feeling the warmth of black marquetry paneling, and touching antique bookcases. They warm at the sight of personal mementos from the Brownings' home.

But this is not the only building in Waco built to fan the flames of love.

ADVENTURES IN HISTORY

America's love affair with Dr Pepper really began in 1904 when the drink was introduced to the nation and to the world at the 1904 World's Fair in St. Louis. Does the jingle "10-2-4" ring a bell? If you want a serious case of nostalgia, stop in at the Dr Pepper Museum where the history of the famous soft drink is told. First introduced as a brown, bubbly drink, it was originally called Waco. Eventually the drink took on the name of a physician named Dr. Charles T. Pepper, a former employer of Dr. Morrison, the founder of Dr Pepper.

In 1880 Dr. Wade B. Morrison moved to Texas and bought Castle's Old Corner Drug Store. He hired a chief pharmacist, Dr. Charles Alderton, who compounded medicines but also enjoyed playing around with formulas and blends of fruit flavors for medicines and fountain drinks. Around 1885, folks began to clamor for one of Alderton's brews, and the company sought a patent for the beverage. With only $1,250 in working capital, Morrison started bottling Dr Pepper and incorporated under the name The Artesian Manufacturing and Bottling Company. A year later the investment had a return of $12,500. In 1906, the company drew up plans for a building that included an artesian well.

Today the sign over the door still proclaims Home of Dr Pepper, but the company moved to Dallas in 1923. The old building has been in the National Register of Historical Places since 1983, but the museum didn't open until 1991. Visitors learn of the origin of the famous drink and the soft drink industry. Bits of information greet visitors at every turn, such as: If you pass acid over marble dust, you get gas carbonation; or the sound of the gas escaping from a bottle causes a loud POP, which led to the drinks being called soda pops.

Dr Pepper has had its share of fanatic fans over the years. Early claims made the drink sound like an aphrodisiac with statements that old men become young and full of vitality. Ads pushed the drink as a tonic, and boomers fondly remember the Dr Pepper 10-2 and 4 commercials. Today museum-goers visit the Old Corner Drug Store and the soda fountain, view a scale model of a 1907 neighborhood, and find early jugs of Dr Pepper syrup. Who doesn't remember stories of prune juice being the base for the old syrup formula? Alas, one more myth from the past to tease us.

Need some pepping up? Miss the taste of the old-time Dr Pepper? Head over to the Dr Pepper bottling plant in downtown Dublin, about ninety miles southwest of Fort Worth, and pick up a case of DP made the old-fashioned way. The Dublin plant is the only one that markets the original formula. Folks travel thousands of miles to pick up a case or two of the original drink. The original formula calls for Imperial pure cane sugar from Sugar Land, Texas—not corn syrup—and, although it costs more to produce, die-hard Pepper fans love it.

The Dr Pepper Bottling Company, established in 1891, is the oldest Dr Pepper bottling plant in the world. Although Drs. Morrison and Alderton may be the founders of the Dr Pepper company, the real Mr. Dr Pepper was Bill Kloster. He started as a bottle sorter for ten cents an hour and, having caught the owner's eye, worked his way up to production manager. After World War II, he married the boss's daughter and, in 1999, took over the company when the owner died. The plant continues to be a testimony to Kloster's passion for the drink. Through his hard work and his refusal to give up the original formula, Kloster turned the company into the tourist attraction it is today. Fans around the world loved him. The media named him Mr. Dr Pepper.

Today, shipments of original Dr Pepper are delivered around the world. If you number among those fans, a trip to the bottling company might be in order. Make sure your car trunk has plenty of room.

ON THE MAP

Located on Interstate 35, Waco marks the center of Texas and is within a three-hour drive of most of Texas. Dublin is located in Erath County in West Central Texas, about ninety miles southwest of Fort Worth.

WEEKEND ADVENTURES

Many historical attractions, such as a row of restored warehouses dating back to 1900 and known as River Square Center, urge visitors to linger. Be sure to visit the Earle-Harrison House and Gardens, a Greek Revival-style mansion, not only to get a feel for how the gentry lived on the Texas frontier, but also to enjoy the botanical garden and grounds. See firsthand how Texans lived in the 1890s at the Governor Bill and Vara Daniels Historic Village and how sharecropping, blacksmithing, and the cotton gin provide a glimpse into early Texas life. The Texas Ranger Law Enforcement Hall of Fame and Museum offers an intimate view of the world-famous law enforcement agency, and the Strecker Museum remains the oldest continuously operating museum in Texas. With a historically restored downtown and five museums, visitors are drawn to the small-town atmosphere and the water walk.

Best Time to Visit

Waco holds the Brazos River Festival, with its Cotton Palace Pageant, in April. If you plan a visit to Dublin, check for the one week in June when Dublin changes its name to Dr Pepper, Texas. Thirty-five hundred Dr Pepper aficionados cram into the town for the Crowning of Pretty Peggy Pepper, the Dr Pepper Carnival, a 10K, 2K–4K Fun Run, and pretelevision-type family entertainment. But don't forget, a Dublin would not be a Dublin without a St. Patrick's Festival. And don't forget the Dublin Rodeo Championship, once home to the World Rodeo Championship that Gene Autry and Everett Colborn made famous.

Adventures in Lodging and Dining

The Cotton Palace is a member of the Historic Accommodations of Texas and is the only state inspected and approved bed and breakfast in the Central Texas area and located within minutes of Waco's historical attractions. Since 1899, Nick's Restaurant has provided Greek cuisine to residents and travelers. For small-town charm, visit Dublin's restaurants with their old-time names of the Buckboard, Old Doc's Soda Shop, and Woody's.

For More Information

Contact the Waco Convention Bureau and Visitor's Center at www.wacocvb.com.

3

In and Around the Dallas–Fort Worth Metroplex

———— DALLAS ————

What the world thinks of as Dallas, evoking images of J. R. Ewing and the TV series, Texans know as the Dallas–Fort Worth Metroplex, two cities combined to create a whole that's larger and more exciting than its components. In addition to the major cities of Dallas and Fort Worth, the metropolitan center includes a series of smaller communities—Addison, Arlington, Farmers Branch, Garland, Grand Prairie, Grapevine, Irving, Mesquite, North Richland Hills, Plano, and Richardson—each retaining its own distinct character.

Dallas has its roots in a simple log cabin that can still be seen today at the Dallas County Historical Plaza. Beginning as a small settlement on the Trinity River, Dallas prospered as settlers came to share John Neely Bryan's vision of a permanent community. After the first train came to town in July 1872, the population more than quadrupled. Through the nineteenth century and into the twentieth, immigrants continued to flow into the city, changing the landscape into one with hotels and other commercial buildings. Today Greater Dallas stands as one of the top commerce centers in the nation.

Dallas's rich heritage and ethnic diversity can be seen in the myriad neighborhoods that make up the city and surrounding suburbs. From the stately mansions of Swiss Avenue to the vibrant urban scene of Deep Ellum, Dallas neighborhoods offer something for everyone. The many parks and lakes—63 within a 100-mile radius—provide recreation opportunities for residents and visitors alike. Downtown walking tours celebrate the city's cultural wealth, highlighting gardens, artwork, and history.

Sadly, one of the events Dallas is most associated with is the assassination of President John F. Kennedy, who was shot to death as his motorcade rolled through the streets of Dallas. The tragedy was compounded when local resident Jack Ruby killed Kennedy's assassin, Lee Harvey Oswald. A reflecting pool and monument stand in Dealey Plaza, commemorating the nation's loss.

Today, with more than two million visitors each year, the Dallas–Fort Worth Metroplex is the top destination in Texas for business travelers and tourists alike.

Adventures in History

For years Texans referred to Dallas as "Big D." Most look to the can-do attitude to account for the city's growth. This spirit pervades every area of commerce that threads through the city's fabric. From the early railroad industry to banking, insurance, and now the computer industries, Dallas has continued to move forward. It's a city with an attitude that can catapult a woman selling cosmetics to other women at home into a major, multimillion dollar industry called Mary Kay Cosmetics. Even the football conglomerate, Dallas Cowboys and the Dallas Cowboys Cheerleaders, made a name for itself the world over. And for a city that faced the worst possible event—the assassination of President John F. Kennedy—Dallas has come through admirably.

But where did this attitude come from? In all likelihood, John Neely Bryan left his imprint forever on Dallas and is probably the genesis of the city's attitude. The first settler in the area, Bryan built a log cabin in 1841. Bryan didn't want to live by himself, so he set about talking up the area. In fact, he may have stretched the truth just a little bit since travelers started pouring in looking for the glorious city they'd heard so much about. You can imagine their disappointment when only a couple of log cabins and a few people welcomed them to the area. But that didn't deter Bryan from his big dreams for Dallas. He even donated land for the county courthouse.

Today you can take a look at a replica of John Neely Bryan's log cabin home and trading post. The Dallas County Historical Plaza, also known as Founders Plaza, sits, with the log cabin, in the heart of downtown against a backdrop of modern skyscrapers.

On the Map

Dallas is found on the Trinity River in Dallas County and is crossed by Interstates 30, 20, 35, and 45.

Weekend Adventures

A good place to start is the Dallas Visitor Information Center in the Dallas County Historical Plaza. Fair Park, home of the State Fair of Texas, includes the Age of Steam Railroad Museum and is open year-round. Other places of historical interest are the Dallas Firefighters Museum, the Sixth Floor Museum, and the Conspiracy Museum.

Waves of Swiss and German immigration impacted the city, and if you're going to spend any time in Dallas, you'll want to explore the historical districts. The Swiss Avenue Historical District is lined with mansions dating back to the early 1900s and is both a Texas Historical Site and a National Register of Historic Places. Nearby is Munger Place Historic District with more than two hundred homes. Of particular note is the Tenth Street Historic District. An intact Freedman's Town, the only one in the nation, Tenth Street has more than two hundred and fifty homes and one cemetery. A trip to Old City Park in the downtown district provides an opportunity for visitors to experience a small village museum consisting of thirty-eight buildings dating from 1840 to 1910. All have been restored to their original condition. Visitors meet the residents, known as first person interpreters, who take on the roles of fictional characters and create a bit of living history drama. Just remember, to them, today is yesterday.

One of the most famous buildings in Dallas is the Texas School Book Depository with the Sixth Floor Exhibit. President Kennedy was shot from the sixth floor of the building. A trip to the Belo Mansion and the Freedman's Cemetery are also in order. A visit to the Arts District includes a walk past the 1902 Cathedral Santuario de Guadalupe and the West End Historic District. Some might be interested in the Mary Kay World Headquarters and Museum. Military aircraft from World War I to Vietnam can be found in Addison at the Cavanaugh Flight Museum, while a trip to Arlington could include a visit to the Johnson Plantation Cemetery and Log Cabins, where two log cabins, built in 1854 and 1858, a one-room schoolhouse, and a barn can be found.

Dallas has had its share of characters. Two of them are Bonnie and Clyde. The two left a deadly trail wherever they went until the fateful day when law enforcement officers pumped 167 rounds of ammunition into their car. Bonnie was twenty-three and Clyde twenty-four when they died. Today, in the city of Dallas, visitors can stop by their gravesites. Don't expect Bonnie and Clyde to be united in death the same way they were united in life. Bonnie Parker's grave can be found in the Crown Hill Cemetery, while Clyde Barrow's site is at the Western Heights Cemetery.

BEST TIME TO VISIT

With more than three million visitors annually, the State Fair of Texas in September and October is a time when many decide to visit the city. The twenty-four days are full of events, entertainment, exhibits, and demonstrations.

ADVENTURES IN LODGING AND DINING

For elegance and history, consider the Adolphus Hotel, built in 1912 by the beer baron Adolphus Busch. Brent Place is a restaurant set in a nine-teenth-century farmhouse, and the Mansion on Turtle Creek is located in the 1920s-era cattle baron's mansion-now-hotel.

FOR MORE INFORMATION

The Dallas Convention and Visitors Bureau is online at www.dallascvb.com.

──── FORT WORTH, TEXAS ────

Although Dallas might be characterized as a boomtown, Fort Worth is clearly a cowtown. Known as the City Where the West Begins, Fort Worth has a history and a tradition steeped in cowboy lore. The city's past, with its myths and legends, draws people from all over the world. One of the number one spots on their itinerary is Billy Bob's Texas, the world's largest honky-tonk. Where else can you find the National Cowgirl Museum and Hall of Fame or the Tarantula Excursion Train? The 1896 train got its name from the way the railway tracks were laid out on the map of Texas—like a big spider.

The city began as a frontier post during the war between the United States and Mexico in 1849, and got its name from Major General William Jenkins Worth. By 1856 the population had increased a great deal, so much so that the town's good citizens had their eye on the county seat of Tarrant County and wondered how they might take the seat away from the town of Birdville. In spite of Birdville's protests and requests for new elections, Fort Worth became the new county seat.

The biggest boost to Fort Worth's growth came with the big cattle drives, particularly that of the Chisholm Trail. Millions of cattle moved through Texas, and the era brought the establishment of Hell's Half Acre, a part of town where gambling, prostitution, saloons, and dance halls reigned. After the cattle came the railroad and even more prosperity. The town grew. But trouble soon plagued the booming town when the Panic of 1873 hit. Overnight folks left the cowtown. Where did all these people go? Dallas. One Dallas newspaper referred to Fort Worth as being "so dead a panther had been seen sleeping unmolested in the streets." Talk about disrespect. Fort Worth would not take this lying down.

And so began the feud that existed for decades between the big, bustling, commerce city of Dallas and the dusty, lively, Wild West town of Fort Worth. After much maneuvering, Fort Worth regained a railroad, and big things happened. Fort Worth grew into Cowtown, a main shipping point for cattle and the home of stockyards and meat packers. Today the Stockyards Historical District is a 125-acre, 15-block square of Wild West tradition and entertainment and leads visitors into a glimpse of the true old west that exemplifies Texas.

But Fort Worth is not just a cowboy city. Known as the Museum Capital of the Southwest, Fort Worth offers a full and lively arts and cultural scene.

ADVENTURES IN HISTORY

Sundance Square in downtown Fort Worth is rich in Western lore and tradition. In fact, the square is named for the Sundance Kid who, with Butch Cassidy, spent some time in the Fort Worth area known as Hell's Half Acre. In 1900, Hell's Half Acre was Fort Worth's version of a red-light district, and there was plenty of action going on, enough to keep the likes of Butch Cassidy and the Sundance Kid occupied. The outlaws had so much fun, they let their guard down and had their picture taken with three other brother-outlaws: Will Carver, Ben "The Tall Texan" Kilpatrick, and Harvey "Kid Curry" Logan. This proved to be a big mistake. Until that moment, the police didn't have any photographs of outlaws.

According to Jerry Adams, author of the online *Trade Token Tales* site, the five outlaws had recently pulled off a bank heist in Winnemucca,

Nevada. Known as the Wild Bunch, they split up and made their way to Fort Worth, Texas, where they had planned to reunite. You would think they wouldn't want to attract any attention. With $33,000 in stolen gold and banknotes, you'd think they would just blow a little steam off in Texas—a place where they had never committed any crimes, a safe haven of sorts. Adams says that the photographer, who was so proud of the group photo, displayed it in the window in time for a passing Wells Fargo agent to recognize one of the outlaws. That little bit of fun cost the outlaws more than $33,000 in stolen money. They'd lost their freedom, but more important, they'd lost their invisibility forever.

On the Map

Accessible from all major highways, Fort Worth is 17.5 miles from the Dallas/Fort Worth International Airport. Located on Interstates 30, 20, and 35W, Fort Worth is a hop-skip-and-a-jump Texas style from Dallas.

Weekend Adventures

There is plenty of history to see in Fort Worth. Learn everything there is about cattle and ranching in Texas and the Southwest at the Cattle Raisers Museum. The Stockyard Station, in the Stockyards National Historic District, provides a cowboy walking tour that includes a behind the scenes look at Billy Bob's, while the Stockyards Collection and Museum tells the Fort Worth story. A trip to the Cattle Baron Mansion brings home the extravagant life of the cattle barons that truly won the West. Every morning the longhorn cattle drives return to the cowtown and are herded down E. Exchange Avenue at 11:30 A.M. and 4:00 P.M. And don't forget the Texas Cowboy Hall of Fame and the Texas Trail of Fame.

Best Time to Visit

The Fort Worth Stock Show and Annual Rodeo is a great draw, but so are the annual Chisholm Trail Roundup in June and the Pioneer Days in

September. Another big favorite is the three-day Red Steagall Cowboy Gathering and Western Swing Festival in October, and the Texas Frontier Forts Muster and Quanah Parker Comanche Pow Wow and Honor Dance is an annual event with reenactors ready and able to give you an accurate experience of life in early Fort Worth. The National Cowboys Museum of Color offers visitors a chance to see learn about the role of African Americans in the American West.

ADVENTURES IN LODGING AND DINING

The Stockyards Hotel in the Stockyards Historic District is listed in the State of Texas Register of Historic Places and the National Trust. Cattle barons and cowboys made this the place to stay in the early years of Fort Worth. The Texas White House Bed and Breakfast, a 1910 Colonial Revival home, is a Fort Worth historical landmark. The White Elephant Saloon, named one of the Best 100 Bars in America by *Esquire Magazine* gives a real taste of Western music and dancing. For something a bit different, try the Carshon's Delicatessen for a kosher-style deli in a restaurant that dates back to 1928. While at the Stockyards, be sure and check out the Cattlemen's Steakhouse.

FOR MORE INFORMATION

The Fort Worth Convention and Visitors Bureau (www.fortworth.com) is in the Sanger Building in Sundance Square.

HOW HOG-WALLOW PRAIRIE
BECAME AN ART DECO SHOWCASE

——— HISTORIC FAIR PARK, DALLAS ———

In 1885 when *Farm and Ranch* publisher Frank Howard proposed a state fair to be held in Dallas, everyone was on board. Inspired by the New

Orleans Exposition held a year earlier, Dallas citizens proved eager to show off their city. The grounds, once described as hog wallow prairie, became Fair Park one year later and the home of the State Fair of Texas. The 227 acres continue to host the State Fair to this day.

The area was completely remodeled in 1935–1936 for the Centennial Exposition in 1936 as a shrine to Texas History and for the Greater Texas and Pan American Exposition that followed. The bill for the remodeling of the Hall of State was $1,200,000—a tremendous amount for the Depression era. The only intact Depression-era exposition site, Fair Park became a National Historic Landmark in 1986. This is the largest collection of Art Deco exposition buildings and art in the nation. The Hall now serves as the home for the Dallas Historical Society and has hosted many events honoring presidents and heads of state.

Today, six million visitors go through the site each year with many attending the three-week State Fair in the fall, but some wonder how many truly appreciate and realize that the level of architecture created on this scale at Fair Park is unrivaled around the world.

ADVENTURES IN HISTORY

Over the years many famous visitors have attended the State Fair and walked the grounds of Fair Park, including Buffalo Bill Cody, Gene Autry, Harry Houdini, and Annie Oakley. In 1909 Comanche Chief Quanah Parker, the son of Comanche Chieftain Peta Nocona and Cynthia Parker, visited the State Fair. Visitors wore badges with the chief's face and the words, "Hear the Big Chief Speak." Quanah called the fair a big show of good things. When he stopped in front of a replica of the Alamo chapel, the Chief said, "Alamo fight was brave like Indian fight. . . . It must make Texas people feel good."

ON THE MAP

Fair Park is two miles east of downtown Dallas near Interstate 30.

BEST TIME TO VISIT

The three-week State Fair in the fall lures many travelers each year.

WEEKEND ADVENTURES

Old City Park, the historical village of Dallas, takes visitors back to the time of 1840–1910. Living history exhibits and historic structures make up the 13-acre village complex. For a look at some of the oldest and most comprehensive heavyweight passenger car collections in America, visit the Age of Steam Railroad Museum in Fair Park where you'll see "Big Boy," the world's largest steam locomotive. The Women's Museum: An Institute for the Future chronicles the lives of women in America and is presented in association with the Smithsonian Institution. One special feature is the 30-foot electronic quilt.

ADVENTURES IN LODGING AND DINING

The Driskell and the Adolphus hotels take travelers back to the past. For a dose of historical ambiance, try Baby Doe's Matchless Mine Restaurant for an old-fashioned Victorian mine and saloon setting.

FOR MORE INFORMATION

Visit the Fair's website at www.bigtex.com. Contact the Dallas Historical Society at www.dallashistory.org/. Also check the Dallas Page at www.thedallaspage.com/ and the Dallas Convention Bureau and Visitors Center at www.dallascvb.com.

FROM OIL BOOM TO ART WALLS

——— BRECKENRIDGE ———

Although originally known as Picketville in 1854, the origin of the town's name is a bit of a mystery. Either the town was named for the post and clay structure of its early dwellings, or perhaps named for an early rancher named Bill Picket. No one knows for sure. However, discussion of the name was made moot a couple of years later when the town became the county seat. At that time it was renamed Breckenridge after John C. Breckinridge, the U.S. senator from Kentucky, and vice president. For some reason, someone altered the spelling of the name, and the town has continued to keep the altered spelling.

The town grew and soon had its own courthouse and newspaper. Then, in the early 1880s, the townspeople built a schoolhouse. Churches, general stores, and a bank promptly sprang up. For several decades, Breckenridge remained a quiet local trading center, but with the discovery of oil and the resulting drilling of Breckenridge field, the town changed.

ADVENTURES IN HISTORY

The great 1920s oil boom shattered the quiet life of the people living in Breckenridge. First one drilling occurred, then another. According to the *Handbook of Texas Online*, thousands of workers and watchers quickly "threw up acres of tents and shacks in the classic oil boomtown manner." More than two hundred oil wells dotted the area, and the small town's population swelled from a mere 1,500 to 30,000. When a town grows this rapidly, it's bound to attract all sorts of people, and Breckenridge was no exception. They trekked in from all over, the gamblers, liquor salesmen, and prostitutes, all ready and willing to lend a hand and make a buck. Because of the rapid influx, the first railroad, the Wichita Falls, Ranger and Fort Worth, quickly appeared. The Cisco and Northeastern rapidly followed. However three years later the boom was over, oil production was down, and many of the people left town. The population decreased even further during the Great Depression. Throughout the 1980s Breckenridge still flourished as a center for petroleum-related industries as well as a retail and shipping center for the rest of the country.

Today, Breckenridge wears another hat as well, one far from the commerce of oil, yet in its own way, connected to that oil-rich time. Breckenridge, the county seat of Stephens County, stepped into the twenty-first century with an artistic flair. The oil-rich boomtown days may be over, but thanks to the impressive talent of Billy Ines, the town has become one massive canvas. The artist, using historic oil boomtown photographs and an airbrush, has taken his talent to the walls of downtown Breckenridge with the blessings of multiple community partnerships. The art is deeply personal to the town because Ines uses the historic Basil Clemons photographs taken during the actual oil boom time in Breckenridge. The Texas Legislature named Breckenridge "The Mural Capital of Texas" in 2001. Young and old enjoy this larger-than-life public art.

On the Map

Breckenridge is located at the intersection of U.S. Highways 180 and 183, four miles east of the Hubbard Creek Reservoir in west central Stephens County. The town is 108 miles from Fort Worth and 145 miles from Dallas.

Weekend Adventures

Visit the Boomtown Breckenridge Murals, winner of the Texas Downtown Association's "Best Public Improvement Project" in 1999. Stop by the Friends of Historic Breckenridge Rest Station to pick up a walking tour brochure of the murals. Take a stroll through town and visit the Swenson Memorial Museum. Stop by the J. D. Sandefer Oil Annex for a look at the Basil Clemons photograph collection of oil boomtown Breckenridge photographs, the basis for the murals, and to see the many pioneer artifacts. View the 1883 Old Courthouse Entrance, said to resemble a Mayan ruin. You'll find it on the lawn of the current courthouse, established in 1926. Look above the door on the rear of the building for homage to the Egyptian "Father of Architecture" Hammurabi. For aviation buffs, check out the Breckenridge Aviation Museum, part of the Confederate Air Force West Texas Wing.

Best Time to Visit

Stephens County's Frontier Days occur around the end of April and the beginning of May and offer everything from horseshoe pitching contests to chuck wagon cook-offs. October is a busy month in Breckenridge as visitors can enjoy music at the Music Festival or attend the Pumpkin Patch party as well as the 50s Fun Day.

Adventures in Lodging and Dining

The Blue Rose Bed and Breakfast invites visitors to recapture the Victorian splendor of a long-gone era, while the Keeping Room Bed and Breakfast offers guests a comfortable place to seek refuge from the hustle and bustle of the outside world. For family fun head out to Jim's Pizza with its indoor playground and dine-in specials, or the L & L Family restaurant. Some other eating establishments include G & P's Diner, Ernie's Spanish Kitchen, Ken's Chicken and Fish, and the Double M Bar-B-Que.

For More Information

To receive a city brochure or for more information, contact the Breckenridge Chamber of Commerce at www.breckenridgetexas/com.

America's Most Beloved Singing Cowboy

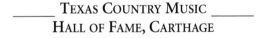

Texas Country Music
Hall of Fame, Carthage

When you take a drive up into the Piney Woods of East Texas, you might want to stop in Carthage, not only the county seat for Panola County but also billed as the best small town in Texas. Spearman Holland named the town in honor of Carthage, Mississippi. "Panola" is an Indian word meaning cotton, the main cash crop of the county in its early days. While the population of 6,664 is small compared to the large Texas metroplexes, this home of country western music is large in its love for music.

Adventures in History

Without a doubt, the star of Carthage and Panola County is the new Texas Country Music Hall of Fame and Tex Ritter Museum. You cannot miss the new museum plaza with the five Texas flags waving brightly and acting as a beacon to any and all country music lovers in the area—and then there's the statue. Ritter fans will recognize the man and his horse, White Flash.

Some might assume Tex Ritter is a Carthage boy, born and bred. Born Woodward Maurice Ritter in 1905 in Panola County's Murvaul, he actually spent his boyhood in Nederland. The future country music movie star began performing in the 1920s. Eventually he caught the eye of two Texans, author J. Frank Dobie and the music folklorist John A. Lomax.

Ritter's fame grew as he played Broadway, crooned country western songs, and became a favorite on radio, TV, and then the movies. Many remember him for the theme music to the popular TV Series *Gunsmoke*. Eventually he became known as America's most beloved singing cowboy. Although Ritter died in 1974, the museum didn't come into being until 1993. When Dorothy Fay, Ritter's wife, donated a truckload of memorabilia to the museum, the board had to look into getting a larger building, and somehow the idea of a hall of fame was born. Today the Hall of Fame and Tex Ritter Museum takes up 13,000 square feet and cost $2.5 million. Each August the Hall of Fame puts on an awards ceremony and show to honor the year's inductees to the Hall of Fame. Past recipients have included Willie Nelson, Gene Autry, and Tanya Tucker.

Another country western favorite from Panola County honored by the Hall of Fame is Gentleman Jim Reeves. With a music career that began in Henderson at a local radio station and ended when he'd reached international acclaim, Reeves is remembered for many songs including the favorite "Mexican Joe" and "Welcome to My World." Unfortunately his career was cut short when he died in a plane crash in 1964. Reeves and his favorite dog, Cheyenne, are buried next to each other in a plot outside Carthage where a granite statue of Reeves has been placed at the site. Every year in April, fans of Reeves gather for the annual Jim Reeves Day hosted by the Hall of Fame.

If you're a lover of country music, a fan of country music stars, and the good old honky-tonk days, the Country Western Texas Hall of Fame and Tex Ritter Museum are for you. Open six days a week, Monday through Saturday, visitors pay a nominal admission fee. Visitors feast their eyes on flashy stage clothes, memorabilia from Ritter's movie days, even Tex's movies. Mementos, recordings, and photographs fill the exhibits as does the tool of a country western singer's trade: the guitar.

ON THE MAP

Located in northeast Texas, 173 miles from Dallas and 42 miles from Shreveport, Louisiana, Carthage is at the intersection of U.S. Highways 59 and 79. The Texas Country Music Hall of Fame and Tex Ritter Museum are at 310 W. Panola Street in Carthage.

WEEKEND ADVENTURES

The new $2.2 million Texas Country Music Hall of Fame and Tex Ritter Museum should be first on the list. The Panola County Heritage Museum can be found in a restored bank building on the square and features antique dolls and an old buggy. A trip to the 1891 Panola County Historical Jail Museum is in order. The old jail is now a historical center and home of the LaGrone Family History Center—the Jail Museum. In fact, the center houses a genealogical library and a mini-law-enforcement and pioneer museum. A fair sized collection of East Texas oral histories can be found in the East Texas Oral History Archive. Three miles east of town visitors can find the Reeves Memorial, a life-sized statue of Jim Reeves.

Lake Murvaul is a few miles southwest of Carthage and offers travelers an opportunity to enjoy the Piney Woods. Visitors enjoy picnicking, fishing, swimming, and boating. The Murvaul Resort and Marine carries groceries, and there is a snack bar for breakfast and lunch.

Best Time to Visit

The main annual event is the Annual Awards Ceremony in August, and there are events planned for Friday and Saturday. Friday evening is the John Rex Reeves Pickin' Party and the County Music Hayride. Saturday night is the awards ceremony. This is a popular event, so order your tickets early. April brings the annual Jim Reeves Jamboree with a sound-alike contest earlier in the day and the tribute in the evening.

Adventures in Lodging and Dining

Panola County has a number of lodgings including the Best Western Inn of Carthage, Boone's Bed and Breakfast, and the Carthage RV campground. Dining fare is simple and ranges from pizza to catfish, from Mexican to Chinese, and includes the Ritters' Chuck Wagon Grill and the Texas Tea Room.

For More Information

The Panola County Chamber of Congress is online at www.carthage texas.com. Call the Tex Ritter Museum at 903-693-6634.

Walk in the Footprints of Giants

——— Dinosaur Valley State Park, Glen Rose ———

Dinosaurs continue to capture the imagination of millions each and every year. For modern dinosaur hunters, some of the best-preserved dinosaur tracks in the world can be found in Dinosaur Valley State Park, Glen Rose, Texas.

Visitors with rich imaginations can easily move back in time and conjure up a vision of a prehistoric era when Dinosaur Valley was little more than tidal flats at the edge of the Gulf of Mexico. Today tracks are likely to be those left by white-tailed deer, armadillos, raccoons, coyotes, bobcats, beavers, and more. Because the dinosaur tracks are located in the Paluxy River bed, it's important to call ahead to check on river conditions.

Adventures in History

First discovered in 1909, the site gained world acclaim in 1940 with New York paleontologist Roland T. Bird's excavation of eighty-seven feet of trackway found in the Paluxy River. The tracks told the story of a carnousaur's ancient hunt. Although the original trackway can be found in New York's American Museum of Natural History, a replica is on display in the state park's interpretive center.

Dinosaur Valley boasts the first sauropod tracks discovered in the world. More than a million years ago, herds of Pleurocoelus, some measuring forty feet in length, walked the river bed in search of food and left their saucer-like and horseshoe-shaped depressions in the mud. These tracks, and some three-toed birdlike prints, are easily seen today in the exposed limestone bed of the Paluxy River that runs through Dinosaur Valley. The two-legged, meat-eating Acrocanthosaurus—predecessor to the mighty Tyrannosaurus rex—traveled up to 25 m.p.h. and could easily run down its prey.

In addition to the tracks, Dinosaur Valley contains two fiberglass dinosaur models built under the commission of the Sinclair Oil Company for the 1964–1965 New York World's Fair Dinosaur Exhibit. Created by artist Paul Jonas, the fiberglass Tyrannosaurus rex and Apatosaurus were later donated to the Texas Parks and Wildlife Department in 1970. According to the department, the long-necked model served as a prototype for Dino the Dinosaur, the Sinclair Oil mascot.

Dinosaur Tracks are easy to find along the Paluxy River in Dinosaur Valley State Park. Vikk Simmons

For those who long for the days of old when swimming holes captured the imaginations of children, visitors won't want to miss the Blue Hole, an old-time swimming hole which averages fourteen feet deep, although in some places it drops to twenty-two feet. Everyone should visit the dinosaur museum located at the park's headquarters where plenty of information about the park, the tracks, and the dinosaurs can be found.

ON THE MAP

Dinosaur Valley is located just northwest of Glen Rose in Somerville County. The park is 85 miles southwest of the Dallas/Fort Worth Metroplex and 75 miles northwest of Waco on State Highway 6 and 220 and U.S. Highway 281.

Weekend Adventures

Although most visitors come to the park initially to see the dinosaur tracks and the park, Park Manager Billy Paul Baker says, "They come back to play in the river and hike the trails." With nearly fifteen miles of trails, there are plenty of things to do. Twelve miles cater to mountain bikers; three miles of trails are reserved for hikers. Backpackers have a number of campsites to choose from. Although there aren't any equestrian facilities, a hundred acres of the park have been set aside for equestrian use. Riders pay only the park entry fee but must bring their own horses. For those who simply want to enjoy the river and view the tracks, the park has a shaded day use area with forty picnic tables and one of the park's two rest rooms.

Nearby, visitors to the area can also stop at the Creation Evidence Museum, Fossil Rim Wildlife Park, Squaw Creek Reservoir, and the towns of Granbury and Glen Rose. For those who'd like to experience a working dinosaur dig site, drive over to the Fort Worth Museum of Science and History in Fort Worth, Texas, and go to the DinoDig, a reproduction of a working site. In addition to being within a few miles of Dinosaur Valley, the town of Glen Rose offers golf, art, shopping, and plenty of wildlife. Glen Rose is located where the Paluxy River merges with Brazos River and began as a trading post in 1849.

Best Time to Visit

Called the Blue Grass Capital of Texas, Glen Rose holds festivals in April and October every year.

Adventures in Lodging and Dining

Overnight guests can use the park's camping loop with forty-six campsites that offer water and electricity, picnic tables, grills, and fire rings. A rest room with showers is also available. For the less hearty, accommodations range from modern hotels to quaint cottages, rustic cabins to bed and breakfasts in nearby Glen Rose and Granbury. Most visitors to the park bring their own food and plan to take advantage of the picnic areas and camping stations. Restaurants can be found in Glen Rose.

FOR MORE INFORMATION

The Dinosaur Valley State Park website www.tpwd.state.tx.us reveals a treasure of information. The Convention and Visitors Bureau of Glen Rose is at www.glenrosetexas.net.

THE MYSTERY OF HISTORY: GRANBURY LORE

——— GRANBURY, TEXAS ———

A favorite town of Texans, Granbury is called the place where Texas history lives. At least that's the claim of the folks of Granbury, Texas, and there's plenty of history, myths, and legends to make the boast valid. Granbury began in 1854. Two groups from Tennessee set out to make their fortune in Texas. The first group, led by "Uncle Tommy" Lambert and Amon Bond, settled across the Brazos River on the west bank. The second group, led by Davy's Crockett's widow, Elizabeth, came to claim the 1,280 acres of land that the state had given to the Alamo hero's heirs.

In 1866 the two Nutt brothers donated forty acres of riverfront property for a new townsite, and the town of Granbury, named for the Civil War's Confederate Gen. Hiram Bronson Granbury, came into being. Granbury's 100-year-old town square celebrated its revival in 1971 and began a huge restoration movement. The courthouse clock tower and the Granbury Opera House were saved, and the entire town square is now listed in the National Register. Granbury has won the Ruth Lester Award for Meritorious Service in Historic Preservation, and the National Trust Foundation has modeled its Main Street Program after Granbury's efforts. *Texas Highways Magazine* named the Victorian courthouse square "The Best Town Square in Texas."

Wagon parked along the road to Fredericksburg. Vikk Simmons

ADVENTURES IN HISTORY

Granbury is rich in history and rich in lore. If a writer had a mind to, he could use Granbury for the setting of two historical mystery novels.

For years the rumor persisted that Jesse James had been buried in the Rash plot at the East End of Granbury Cemetery. DNA tests finally confirmed the existence of Jesse's body lying in a grave in Missouri. The Granbury residents say not true. After an exhumation and DNA tests in 1995, controversy still existed as noted by Betty Dorsett Duke in her book *Jesse James Lived and Died in Texas*. Duke brought up charges of false material and, therefore, false results. In 2000, historian Bud Hardcastle received permission for a second exhumation, but tests were done on the wrong body, and the mystery remains to this day.

Historians still say Jesse James is buried in Missouri. Granbury lore suggests he staged his death and moved to Granbury.

A second historical debate swirls around the Lincoln assassin John Wilkes Booth. Conspiracy advocates are sure the government whisked him out of the way and did a witness protection-type move by helping him change names and take on the role of a saloonkeeper by the name of John St. Helen. The controversy arose when St. Helen thought he was dying and supposedly confessed his true identity to a Catholic priest. Upon recovery, St. Helen denied it all and left town. So this controversy remains as well.

On the Map

Granbury is located 65 miles southwest of Dallas or 30 miles southwest of Fort Worth, on U.S. 377 and Texas Highway 144.

Weekend Adventures

The Hollywood Movie Museum and Antique Mall, also home to the National Museum of Communications, makes for a nice change of pace. Acton State Park, the smallest state park in Texas, includes the grave of Elizabeth Crockett in the Acton Cemetery. Built in 1914, the Railroad Depot draws many travelers. The Jail and Hood County Historical Museum is housed in the Old Granbury Jail built in 1885, and the historic Granbury Opera House offers local and regional productions. Some say the Opera House is haunted. Other museums include the 1914 Railroad Depot Museum and the Hood County Museum. For a trip into the recent history, take in a movie at the Brazos Drive-in Theater, an authentic 1950s drive-in movie theater. Take a ride on Zion's Dream Paddlewheeler or a dinner cruise around the lake.

Best Time to Visit

There are always wonderful things to see and do in Granbury. However, if you prefer to tie in a visit with festivals and celebrations, try these: March for the Annual General Granbury Birthday Celebration and Bean and Rib Cookoff; April's Great Race of Texas; the Fourth of July Parade and Arts and Crafts Festival; the Harvest Moon Arts and Crafts Festival in October; and December's Candlelight Tours.

Adventures in Lodging and Dining

The Captain's House on the Lake Bed and Breakfast and 1909 Guest House is the only historically registered bed and breakfast on Lake Granbury and voted among the top fifteen bed and breakfasts in North America for friendliness. For what *Texas Highways* describes as "Victorian Splendor," stop by the National Register's, turn-of-the-century Chaska House Bed and Breakfast. The Old Rosemary Mansion on Main Street "has been featured in *D Magazine, Texas Highways* and Johnny Boggs's *Pampered Cowboy*." Another famous citizen of Granbury lends his name to the Billie Sol Estes Bed and Breakfast and Memorabilia. Convicted in 1963 for mail fraud and conspiracy, the memory of the "King of the Texas Wheeler-Dealer Deals" is still alive in the museum operated by Billie Sol's daughter, Pam, and opened in 1995. Victorian elegance abounds in Granbury, and there is plenty of lodging for everyone's taste.

Dining on the square is easy enough with all the restaurants, including tearooms, cantinas, and Cajun cafes. The 1893 landmark Nutt House Hotel and bed and breakfast has been renovated for modern amenities and has a gourmet restaurant.

For More Information

Check with the Granbury Convention Bureau and Visitor's Center at www.granburytx.com/.

A Small Town, an Outlaw, and a Mystery

——— Hico ———

Founded in 1856 on Honey Creek, Hico borders the Bosque River and promises the perfect spot for relaxation and a real Texas experience.

Texas Monthly Magazine selected Hico as the most authentic town in Texas. But is this idyllic western town the stage for a raging historical mystery? One theory is that on a July night in 1881, Pat Garrett killed Billy the Kid. But did he?

ADVENTURES IN HISTORY

Sometime in the mid-1900s "Brushy" Bill Roberts showed up in North Central Texas and eventually settled in Hico. He ended his days in 1950 when he suffered a heart attack on the way to the Hico post office and died four days before his ninety-first birthday.

That should have been the end of the story, but Brushy Bill did not live out his last days in peace. Two years earlier, in 1948, an investigator named William Morrison arrived in town. During the course of settling an estate for a client, Morrison learned that Billy the Kid was still alive and living in Texas. Morrison's search led him to Hico and to Brushy Bill where he discovered that Billy the Kid did not die at Fort Sumner after all. Instead, Morrison believed Pat Garrett only claimed the man he shot was Billy to collect the five-hundred-dollar reward and enhance his reputation. Billy escaped to Mexico.

But why would an infamous outlaw, long considered dead, risk exposure by returning to the states and settling in Hico? Bob Hefner, local newsman and printer, authored a souvenir booklet in honor of Hico's hundredth Old Settler's Reunion that detailed the story of Brushy Bill Roberts and claims he has the answer. Billy the Kid's real name was William Henry Roberts. As a young boy, he spent three years in Hico living on his father's homestead outside of town. In the end, Hefner believes the outlaw returned to Hico to die because he considered Hico home.

Brushy Bill denied the accusations, but eventually Morrison wore him down. Brushy Bill asked Morrison to end it all and help him get a pardon. If successful, Brushy Bill would confess. All he wanted was a pardon and his privacy. Unfortunately New Mexico's governor thought differently and declined the request. The story generated a lot of press at the time. After Brushy Bill's death, Morrison and El Paso historian C. L. Sonnichsen published Brushy Bill's story in the book *Alias Billy the Kid.*

Despite Morrison's book, folks continued to question Bushy Bill's story. Later, Hefner discovered an interview in 1950 by an El Paso reporter with a Mrs. Mardle Ables, who claimed she had seen and talked to Billy the Kid the day before, and that he was using the alias of Ollie Roberts, nicknamed Brushy Bill. Determined to solve the mystery once and for all, Hefner joined forces with William Tunstill, and together they claim to have the evidence that proves Old Brushy was Billy the Kid.

Hico has embraced its infamous son, Brushy Bill Roberts, and celebrates the real Billy the Kid with an annual *Billy the Kid Day.* Certainly Billy the Kid is a part of history, but is he a part of Hico history? See for yourself: the legend lives on in Hico's Billy the Kid Museum on Pecan Street. In W. C. Jameson's book, *Billy the Kid: Beyond the Grave,* the discussion continues. Evidence is included that is revealed through the use of new technology in photo imaging.

ON THE MAP

Hico is located 85 miles southwest of the Dallas/Fort Worth Metroplex and 75 miles northwest of Waco on State Highway 6 and 220 and U.S. Highway 281.

WEEKEND ADVENTURES

In addition to the Billy the Kid Museum, this turn-of-the-century town has a lot to offer with all the antique shops, leather and knife craftsmen, great restaurants, free Saturday night music, and carriage rides. There's even a hand-crafted chocolate shop. For a frontier experience with horseback riding and campouts, hay rides, saddlebag lunches, and sunset champagne rides, visit the Texas Hoedown at the Timber Creek Ranch. Smooth Water Ranch has an outdoor bandstand and musicals year-round.

BEST TIME TO VISIT

In July Hico celebrates Old Settler's Reunion, a Hico tradition since 1882 that offers a look at the ranch life experience and features a parade, carnival, musical entertainment, carriage rides, cowboy poetry, and more. Smooth Water Ranch holds its annual Fourth of July *Americana Jam*, two days and nights of camping, music, and fun for the entire family.

ADVENTURES IN LODGING AND DINING

If you love antiques, the Railroad Bed and Bath is for you. Stop at the Koffee Kup, a roadside café, for fried onion rings, hamburgers the size of plates, and their claim of a to-die-for coconut pie. In need of a margarita and Mexican food? Try Jersey Lilly's on Pecan Street and take advantage of their free horse-drawn buggy rides on Saturday nights. For live entertainment, there's Rusty's Outback at 2nd and Elm Street.

MORE INFORMATION

Contact the Hico, Texas, Chamber of Commerce and Civic Club, at www.hico-tx.com.

A TINY TOWN PRODUCES A KING

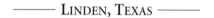

—— LINDEN, TEXAS ——

In 1852 Major Wood probably didn't expect his name to become synonymous with the town's main industry. Wood named the town of Linden for his old home in Tennessee. He soon realized, as many new towns developed in the Red River valley, the pine and hardwood trees of the area were in great demand. Although in Linden's early years this seat of Cass County saw both lumber and syrup mills flourish, the town's timber became its mainstay. The lumber industry remained viable until the

Great Depression forced the close of many of Linden's businesses and the population shrank to about 1,000.

After World War II, business rebounded, and the town grew at a slow pace. Today Linden's population has increased to over 2,000 with the economy concentrated on farming, lumber, oil, and tourism.

ADVENTURES IN HISTORY

Music must be infusing the air in the small East Texas town of Linden. A number of nationally known musicians call Linden home, including Gene Autry's band and the Cass County Boys. Despite its size, Linden has also produced at least three notable musicians: Scott Joplin, Aaron Thibeau Walker, and Don Henley.

The "King of Ragtime" music, Scott Joplin, was born near Linden in 1868. After spending several years playing in saloons and brothels, he moved to St. Louis where he led in the development of the ragtime music genre. In the 1890s Joplin wrote the "Maple Leaf Rag," quickly followed by his famous composition "The Entertainer." Most unusual is his musical creation "The Great Crush Collision," inspired by the crash in Texas of two locomotives. In the early 1900s he moved to New York City and produced "Treemonisha," the first grand opera composed by an African American and for which, in 1976 many years after his death, he received the Pulitzer Prize. He also received belated recognition when the motion picture *The Sting* won an Academy Award for its film score.

Linden is the birthplace of Aaron Thibeau "T-Bone" Walker, the first blues singer to use the electric guitar and known as the Daddy of the Blues. Filled with a combination of wanderlust and love of music, T-Bone Walker ran away from grade school to join a medicine show. By the time he was ten years old, he could be found dancing at the conclusion of his uncle's string band shows. In 1929 he won an amateur show, and first prize was a week with Cab Calloway's band. T-Bone was on his way. He finally obtained record contracts, recording such hits as

"T-Bone Shuffle" and "Call It Stormy Monday (But Tuesday's Just as Bad)." Then, when the popularity of the blues was fading, T-Bone got a break singing with Count Basie. In his musical career he worked with many greats such as Cab Calloway, Ma Rainey, Les Hite, as well as Count Basie. The blues genre is all the richer today as T-Bone's music influenced B. B. King along with many other vocalists and musicians.

Although Don Henley of the Eagles was born in Gilmer, Texas, he grew up in Linden, where his mother still resides. The Eagles meld country, folk, R&B, rock, and pop, creating a distinctly American musical style. This innovative and commercially successful band has sold over 100 million albums worldwide. In the course of their decade-long career, the group also won four Grammy awards.

Henley embarked on a solo career in the early 1980s. This endeavor has also met with a great deal of success. In 1982 he was nominated for three Grammys and won Best Rock Vocal (Male) for his hit song "The Boys of Summer." Henley is a remarkable composer as well, creating a unique sound by combining the best of pop and country. A few of his best known hits are "Lyin' Eyes," "Hotel California," "New Kid in Town," and "Desperado."

Along with his music career, Henley is an environmental activist who founded the non-profit Caddo Lake Institute that underwrites ecological education and research. Since Henley spent his early years around the Texas wetlands, CLI, as part of the Caddo Lake Coalition, helps protect the Texas wetland. In the late 1990s, Henley returned to East Texas with his wife and two children and in April of 2001 served as Grand Marshall of the Wildflower Trails Parade. He continues to pursue his music career successfully with the release of his album "Inside Job."

Visitors can expect the musical story to continue with the development of several new projects. One is the Texas Rock and Roll Hall of Fame. Another, the Cass County Musicians Museum, will house memorabilia from Don Henley, Scott Joplin, and T-Bone Walker. The East Texas 59 Roadtrip, a newly formed coalition based on musical heritage, plans to be active in towns from Carthage through Texarkana. Holding monthly concerts, Music City Texas Theater expands Linden's musical vision. If you love music, visit Linden, Texas.

On the Map

Linden is located in the northeast corner of Texas on U.S. 59 in the south central portion of Cass County. It's forty miles south of Texarkana, about 150 miles east of the Dallas–Fort Worth Metroplex, and 250 miles north of Houston.

Weekend Adventures

To tap into a time prior to the Civil War, check out the Cass County Courthouse built in 1860. Made of brick in the classical revival style, it was built before the war and remodeled in 1900 and 1933. If music is calling, see some of the greatest musicians in the Music City Texas Theater. Past guests include Riders in the Sky and T. Graham Brown. Plans for the Music City Texas Theater's activities include the presentation of community theater and educational workshops in the fields of music and the arts. Take a trip to the area known as the "Gateway to the Lake." With a short drive, visitors can find Wright Patman Lake, Lake O' the Pines, or Caddo Lake replete with various outdoor recreation. Travel a little further and view the historic river port of Jefferson located thirteen miles south.

Best Time to Visit

Ever since April 1970, the Wildflower Trails of Texas Festival has been held in Linden and several nearby cities. Check out the schedule of events that ends with the grand finale on the last week weekend of April. Linden has a parade, craft booths, and various other activities on that Saturday and usually includes the Cass County Championship Rodeo. If the timing of the festival isn't right, travel to Linden in April anyway to enjoy the thousands of naturally occurring wildflowers throughout the region. Travelers can also enjoy the Linden Market Fest held every Friday evening on the courthouse lawn.

ADVENTURES IN LODGING AND DINING

Linden is only a 15- or 20-minute drive from sixty-five bed and breakfasts. It's also thirteen miles from historic Jefferson, known as the Bed and Breakfast Capital of Texas. The Inn of Jefferson is located three-fourths of a mile from the historic downtown district. Colonel Hughes Lodging bed and breakfast and the Honeysuckle Rose bed and breakfast are located in Hughes Springs and Holly Hill, only eleven miles west of town. Atlanta and Queen City also have several bed and breakfasts. If outdoors is a preference, try Linden RV Park–School Lane, owned by the City Parks Board.

In Linden, eat at Cindy's Café on courthouse square or start your day with breakfast every day at Cinci's Candies & Café. For a beautiful view from the top of a hill while you eat, go to Vaughan's Catfish. Visitors can find Mexican Cuisine at El Inca, and Juanita's Kitchen is just north of the courthouse. For good old-fashioned barbecue, drive out on U.S. 59 to Tommy's Bar-B-Q between Linden and Atlanta. There are also numerous eating establishments fifteen minutes north in Atlanta. In Hughes Springs try Honeysuckle Rose on Ward Street, Gatsby's, or Wildflower Restaurant on the east end of town.

FOR MORE INFORMATION

Contact the Linden Area Chamber of Commerce by e-mail at ledc@linden-wireless.com.

JAMES BOWIE: THE MAN, THE MYTH, AND THE LEGEND

——— TEXARKANA, TEXAS ———

Texans are proud of their heritage and their towns and love to boast, and Texarkana is no exception. Its Chamber of Commerce proudly displays the motto, "Texarkana . . . Where Life is So Large It Takes Two States."

Texarkana is actually two cities located in two states, so the city boasts a second motto, "Twice As Nice."

Texarkana traces its early beginnings to around 1840 in the old Caddo territory. Later, a post office formed in Lost Prairie about 15 miles from present Texarkana, railroads pushed through, and the Red River Bridge opened in 1874. The naming of the city remains unclear. Some claim the surveyor for the Iron Mountain Railroad right-of-way wrote Tex-Ark-Ana on a board and nailed it to a tree. He told folks it was to be the name of the town to be built there. Or perhaps he just figured he was standing where three states met, so he named the city after those states—Texas, Arkansas, and Louisiana. Whatever the story, Texarkana is unique since the city is divided by a man-made line, State Line Avenue, instead of a natural barrier, and claimed by two states, Texas and Arkansas.

A Texan by adoption, James Bowie lived mostly in San Antonio, and Texans are happy to claim this feisty hero. Although he fought for Texas, he became a national hero as well. The western half of Texarkana lies in Bowie County. Even though he made the first one of his famous knives in Washington, Arkansas, visitors to Texarkana today can view a large sculpture of Bowie gripping a rifle and Bowie knife. The statue stands as a memorial to Texarkana's vision and spirit. Welcome to Texarkana where the charm of the South meets the spirit of the West.

ADVENTURES IN HISTORY

Many historians believe that not James but his brother Rezin invented the Bowie knife. Certainly Jim Bowie's wild antics with the Bowie knife are what made both him and the knife famous. During one bloody incident, Bowie used one of the knives to disembowel a man.

Born in 1796, James Bowie grew up on a plantation in Louisiana where his parents, who bought and sold slaves along with growing cotton and sugar cane and raising livestock, were also reported to be the largest slave owners in the area. He liked hunting and fishing, and tradition says he caught and rode wild horses and alligators and trapped bears. He is reported to have been around six feet and 180 pounds with a fierce temper.

After the War of 1812, Bowie and his brother Rezin traded in slaves, buying them from the pirate Jean Lafitte, a dangerous act since, although owning slaves was perfectly legal, buying and selling them was not. Rich from his exploits in sugar milling, speculation, and slave trading, Bowie had no difficulty winning the hand of Ursula Veramendi, the daughter of the governor of the province of Texas. Bowie became a Mexican citizen, and they settled in San Antonio. An adventurer, Bowie was not often at home and cultivated friendships with Indians to help in his search for the silver and gold he believed to be hidden in Texas. Accounts vary, but he and his men also fought brutal battles with the Indians several times. Some claim he even found the San Saba mines, also called the Bowie mines, in what is now central Texas. During this time, Bowie fought in various uprisings and town battles, taking the side of whoever he felt would further his fortunes as a land speculator.

He and his wife might have had one, two, or even no children. As in many tales from the old west, the history is muddied, and sources disagree. What is certain is that tragedy struck. While Bowie was on a business trip, the entire Veramendi household was killed in a cholera epidemic. Bowie, ill with yellow fever himself, didn't know of the deaths until later. After the loss of his family, Bowie began drinking heavily. During this time, Texas was in turmoil, and Bowie always seemed to be in the thick of it. At one point, after communications had ended between Mexico and Texas, Bowie took a group of Texas militia to San Antonio and grabbed a stack of muskets from the Mexican armory. From that time on until the battle at the Alamo, Bowie recruited men to fight, created diversions, and led forces in the war for Texas independence. Never interested in formal command, he was in charge of volunteer armies. He shared leadership in Bexar with Commander William Barret Travis. Even though he was sick with what was most likely pneumonia and confined to his cot, he fought at the Alamo until the end, dying from several shots in his head.

Was Jim Bowie, as some claim, a drunk, a swindler, a slave trader, and a troublemaker—vicious when his temper was roused? Or, as others state, did he have a noble character? Was he a man who was cultivated, kind and pleasant to women, a man who would quickly come to a defenseless man's aid? Probably all of the above. One thing is certain, the tales of his exploits reveal a man with a great deal of charisma who fought hard, drank hard, and played hard, but he was also a man who died a hero with stories and legends about him still making the rounds to this day.

On the Map

Texarkana is composed of two cities with the same name and is located at the junction of Interstate 30 and U.S. Highways 59, 67, 71, and 82 in extreme northeastern Texas on the Texas-Arkansas border.

Weekend Adventures

Join the multitude of other visitors and stand in front of the post office and plant one foot in Texas, one in Arkansas. There are many architectural treasures in Texarkana. On Pine Street, visitors will find the Ace of Clubs House, a 22-sided house built on winnings from a poker game. All the rooms represent different periods in history. The Augustus Garrison Historical Home, built in 1895, is a late Victorian home with gingerbread trim, period furnishings, and antiques. The Draughn-Moore House, 1884, has a unique octagonal rotunda making it an interesting place to visit. The Mansion on Main, a Texas State historical site, is filled with authentic furnishings and is one of only three Texas Medallion recipients in Texarkana. You can join a tour, but you must make an appointment. Finally, listed on the National Register of Historic Places, the Little Victorian House, a Texas Historic Landmark, was paid for in cash from gambling money and is filled with Victorian and Western artifacts.

Other areas of interest include the Old Rialto Building, Regional Arts Center, Union Station, Rose Hill Cemetery, Museum of Regional History, Regional Arts Center, and the Texarkana Historical Society and Museum, erected in 1879 and listed in the National Register of Historic Places.

BEST TIME TO VISIT

There are many events and festivals in Texarkana and many times of the year to enjoy them. Some of the events include Sparks in the Park on the first Saturday in July and Monroe's Bluegrass Festivals on Memorial and Labor Day Weekends. For two days of fun that feature live music, art, and lots of kid's activities, join visitors and locals at the Quadrangle Festival on the first weekend after Labor Day. For nine days beginning the second weekend after Labor Day, folks flock to Texarkana for their famous Four States Fair and Rodeo.

ADVENTURES IN LODGING AND DINING

Aside from the usual assortment of hotels and motels, Texarkana offers a quaint Victorian Inn located downtown. Relax at the Mansion on Main Bed & Breakfast of Texarkana. Enjoy a memorable experience at this bed and breakfast filled with Victorian parlors furnished in antiques. Get pleasure from a full southern breakfast at their nine-foot walnut table and be sure to savor the specialty of the house, baked filled French toast. If steak is on the menu, try the Texas Roadhouse—Epinions.com gives it a four-star review. Steaks are hand cut and side items made from scratch. The motto is "Legendary Food Through Legendary Service Through Legendary People," and the restaurant brags that its portions are so large that the tables do the tipping. There are several ethnic restaurants including Mexican, Italian, and Japanese. For something different, go to Springer's Smokehouse for Basque food. Barbecue is also available in town.

FOR MORE INFORMATION

For further information contact the Texarkana Chamber of Commerce by e-mail at chamber@texarkana.org for information and photos, or go to the website www.texarkana.org.

4

In and Around Houston

The world views Houston—and Texas—as a city of rough and tumble cowboys, rodeo and livestock shows, oil and gas, but many Americans find Houston synonymous with space. Although Houstonians have long called Houston the Bayou City, today the Greater Houston Convention and Visitors Bureau calls Houston "SpaceCity USA." Whatever the moniker, Houston—the fourth largest city in the nation—is both a cultural and an international city.

On August 26, 1836, the Allen brothers, Augustus C. and John K., bought six thousand plus acres of land along Buffalo Bayou for five thousand dollars. The battle of San Jacinto had occurred four months earlier, and the brothers sought to honor General Sam Houston by naming the town after the new war hero. The ambitious brothers sold the land for one dollar per acre and advertised throughout the country. The flow of people into the city began—and has yet to end.

The city's name is not the only link to the birthing of the Republic of Texas. The San Jacinto Battleground State Historical Park marks the spot where the revolution ended in 1836. Many visitors witness the annual reenactment of the eighteen-minute battle held every April. A quick search through the Texas Historical Commission's Texas Historic Sites

Gazebo in Sam Houston Park, Houston. Vikk Simmons

Atlas for Harris County reveals 711 records: 241 National Register list-ings, 1 courthouse, 28 museums, and 270 historical markers. Sites in-clude the spot where Sam Houston led the Texas army across Buffalo Bayou using a raft built of wood taken from Isaac Batterson's house. The ensuing march led to the victory at San Jacinto, April 21, 1836.

Two historical districts are of special note to visitors. Freedman's Town Historic District, traditionally known as Houston's Fourth Ward, com-prises forty blocks west of downtown Houston. The district began as the Freedman's town settlement and is one of the oldest and most important black communities in Houston. In the heart of downtown Houston, travelers the world over visit the Heritage Society at Sam Houston Park, the city's only outdoor, interactive historic museum and park. The nineteen-acre park has a number of early dwellings and a church.

Today, Houston continues to be at the heart of the nation's history and no example is more reflective of the city's importance nationally than NASA's Johnson Space Center.

ADVENTURES IN HISTORY

Say "NASA" and people think Houston, Mission Control. The crackled sound of communication between NASA's Mission Control and the many space missions is encapsulated in the historic moment when the world heard Neil Armstrong's famous "The Eagle has landed."

On May 25, 1961, then President John F. Kennedy declared the United States would land a man on the moon and return him safely to the earth by the end of the decade. Less than four months later, Houston became the site for the new Manned Spacecraft Center. The Center, renamed to honor President Johnson after his death in 1973, officially opened its first building in 1963. Four years later, Neil Armstrong and Buzz Aldrin landed on the moon, and NASA met President Kennedy's challenge, opening up a new era in the nation's history.

Today the Johnson Space Center (JSC) has guided more than one hundred shuttle missions and serves as the headquarters for the International Space Station. While the JSC is closed to visitors, travelers can view the facility from a tram or attend the annual open house. With an estimated attendance of 130,000, there are some lines; however, the official Johnson Space Center visitor center, Space Center Houston, easily accommodates the flow of visitors.

Space Center Houston is open year-round and is not a part of NASA. Space Center Houston is separate and is non-profit, owned and operated by the Manned Space Flight Education Foundation, Inc. It does not receive any federal funding. The JSC's visitor program ended in 1992 when Space Center Houston opened. By keeping in close contact with

NASA, the center's creators have ensured the most accurate experience. Each attraction is self-guided so you can spend as much time or as little in each area as desired. Generally, you should plan to spend four to six hours. The center includes Space Center Plaza, Kids Space Place, Starship Gallery, Mission Status Center, NASA Tram Tour, Space Center IMAX Theater, the Feel of Space, Spacetrader Gift Shop, and special exhibits and events.

ON THE MAP

Houston is 160 miles from Austin, 210 miles from San Antonio, 238 miles from Dallas. Use Interstate 10 or Highways 45 or 59. The Johnson Space Center and Space Center Houston are located 26 miles south of downtown Houston in Clear Lake on NASA Road One.

WEEKEND ADVENTURES

The George Ranch Historical Park, located southwest of Houston, is a working ranch and museum, and the Buffalo Soldiers National Museum is fast becoming a favorite attraction. For a glimpse into the cowboy life, go to the American Cowboy Museum on Taylor-Stephenson Ranch, which has a ranch that has been in the family for six generations and preserves the Western heritage of African Americans, Hispanics, Native Americans, and women. Museum-goers can spend days traveling up and down the Museum district taking in all that Houston offers. The Museum of Printing History's collection includes antique printing presses, hands-on demonstrations, and collections of rare books, prints, and historic newspapers. The Barbara Bush Gallery of Documents contains, among many other things, early printing related to the history of the Republic of Texas. To pay respects to the last president of the Republic of Texas, Dr. Anson Jones, and many other famous persons, visit Glenwood Cemetery on Washington Avenue.

BEST TIME TO VISIT

Plenty of fairs, festivals, and celebrations occur in Houston year-round, with the annual Houston Livestock Show and Rodeo and the Houston International Festival two of the largest. In addition to Space Center's annual Open House, the Ballunar Liftoff Festival, the largest hot-air balloon event in Texas, is usually held on the same weekend.

ADVENTURES IN LODGING AND DINING

Houston has every kind of lodging imaginable. The Sam Houston Hotel and the Magnolia Hotel are both located in historic structures. Major hotels include the Four Seasons, Hyatt Regency Houston, and the new Inn at the Ball Park. The Warwick, built in 1925, is located in the museum district. Angel Arbor Bed and Breakfast is located in the historic Heights District. The Patrician Bed and Breakfast is in the museum district.

Former Houston Rocket's Clyde Drexler's restaurant, Drexler's World Famous BBQ & Grill, recently relocated into a newly renovated warehouse minutes from the downtown Toyota Center. Downtown Aquarium not only offers "a world of marinelife," but also restaurants and amusements. A trip to Houston's Galleria, "the Southwest's premier shopping center," reveals more than 470 shops and restaurants. A 20-mile trip to the Kemah Boardwalk includes specialty shops, midway games and rides, and restaurants such as Landry's Seafood House, The Flying Dutchman, and Joe's Crab Shack. Vic and Anthony's Steakhouse has not only fine steaks but also a piano lounge and bar.

FOR MORE INFORMATION

Houston's Visitors Center (www.houston-spacecityusa.com) is the largest in the United States and offers many things, including museum-quality exhibits and more than 10,000 brochures, books, magazines, flyers, and other information. Also, check the Greater Houston Visitor's

Bureau and Convention Center website (www.houston-guide.com). Contact Space Center Houston (www.spacecenter.org) for more information.

THE TALK OF HEMPSTEAD: ELISABET NEY AT LIENDO

———— LIENDO PLANTATION, HEMPSTEAD, TEXAS ————

Today Hempstead, Texas, is known as the Watermelon Capital of the World and is the County Seat for Waller County. Established in 1856, Hempstead became a railroad town and connected Houston and Texas Central Railroads. In its early years after the Civil War, the town carried the moniker of Six-Shooter Junction. By the turn of the century, the violence had reached fever pitch with the shooting death of U.S. Congressman John Pinckney, his brother, and two others. The unexpected gunfight occurred when the congressman met with local prohibitionists and drew national attention. According to reports the four men were dead within two minutes of the heckling that then escalated into the shoot-out. Afterwards the wall of the courthouse told the story with more than 75 bullet holes.

Located fifty miles outside Houston, the lure of watermelons and wildflowers draws visitors to the area every year. Another big draw is Liendo Plantation just outside Hempstead and 45 minutes from downtown Houston. As one of Texas's earliest cotton plantations, Liendo is a Texas Historic Landmark and is listed on the National Register of Historic Places. In its day Liendo was "the social center of Texas receiving and lavishly entertaining early Texas dignitaries."

ADVENTURES IN HISTORY

The richness of Liendo's history skyrocketed when Elisabet Ney, considered one of the most colorful and influential women in early Texas history, and her physician, scientist, and philosopher husband, Edmund

Montgomery, purchased the plantation in 1873 for $10,000. The couple spent two decades at Liendo, originally called the Groce's Plantation. Self-sufficient, the plantation produced everything the inhabitants needed except for buttons. Those had to be imported.

Even by the time Ney and her husband moved in, the plantation had earned a reputation as a landmark. The original owner, José Justo Liendo, had been assigned the land from an original Spanish land grant. In 1853 Leonard Waller Groce built the plantation with slave labor and bricks made out of Brazos red clay. The plantation included a school-house, and what was then called a bachelors' hall to accommodate those guests who streamed between Houston-Galveston and Austin and used the plantation as a stopover. During the Civil War, the plantation hosted two training camps: Camp Groce for infantry and Camp Carter for Cavalry. An internment camp housing prisoners from the Battle of Galveston and a hospital were also erected. But for the gracious hospitality extended to George Armstrong Custer and his wife during the times immediately after the war, Liendo might have been burned to the ground. Custer disregarded the orders to burn the plantation when he left.

When Ney and Montgomery took up residence, they changed the plantation's name to Liendo. Ney, one of the first professional sculptors in Texas and a pioneer in the development of the art in Texas, had been the first woman sculpture student accepted in the Munich Art Academy. Bismarck, Garibaldi, and King Ludwig II of Bavaria numbered among those she modeled during her early years. In the years after her life at Liendo, she sculpted "the great men of frontier Texas." Visitors to the national and state capitals can still see the life-size figures.

Liendo was the scene of great grief for Ney and her husband. Shortly after their arrival in Liendo, their son Arthur became ill, apparently from diphtheria. Despite her efforts to care for him, the little boy died. Grief-stricken, Elisabet made a small plaster cast of her baby's face and then cremated the child herself in one of Liendo's fireplaces. Visitors to Liendo today are told of the story and shown the exact fireplace and the room where the cremation occurred.

Quite the eccentric, Elisabet became the talk of Hempstead. When she and Edmond secretly married, she had promised never to tell. She retained her surname for the rest of her life, so many thought her children had been born out of wedlock. She often dressed in Grecian robes and knee boots and was known to stand on a wooden sledge and be pulled by a team of mules as her other son, Lorne, drove. Although Elisabet is reputed to have stood on the upper veranda and stated, "This is where I shall live and die," she did leave the plantation for a number of years and garnered great fame in Austin. However, at her death she was returned to Liendo by train. As the story goes, Lorne placed the death mask of young Arthur in the coffin with her. She and her husband are both buried at Liendo.

Today, a tour of the plantation offers a glimpse into this serene paradise occupied by Elisabet and her husband and a view of some of their personal items. The plantation also preserves a glimpse into the history of slave plantations, but remember that the plantation is still an actual home to those who live there today. In 1960 the Deterings bought the plantation and began a 10-year restoration. The plantation is open for tours the first Saturday of most months with a nominal admission fee.

On the Map

Liendo is at the crossroads of Highway 290 and FM 1488 outside Houston.

Weekend Adventures

If you want a taste of early Texas during the Civil War, then visit Liendo Plantation in November during the annual Civil War Weekend. You'll have a chance to experience how the Victorian Era dealt with the hardships of war that occurred during the Civil War. Rain or shine, the event happens. The 3rd and 11th Texas Regiments of cavalry and the Gulf States Living History Association sponsor this three-day event. The reenactors demonstrate spinning; weaving; quilting; blacksmithing; soap, broom, and furniture making, as well as life at the camps during the war. Dances, home tours, and music by an orchestra and a brass band add to the experience.

While you're in the vicinity, stop by Hempstead and the Union Prisoner of War Cemetery–Austin Branch. A historical marker is at the site located at Sorsby Road. In the spring, a drive through the area will reveal carpets of wildflowers. April brings the Old South Festival held on the third weekend at Liendo plantation, the annual 4th of July

Civil War reenactors take a break during the annual Civil War Weekend at Liendo Plantation. Vikk Simmons

celebration with fireworks occurs in Hempstead Park, and the Watermelon Festival is celebrated on the third Saturday of July. With a parade, watermelon seed spitting contests, and more, the festival promises great fun. In addition to the Civil War reenactment at Liendo traditionally held the weekend before Thanksgiving, Hempstead puts on a Festival of Lights on the second Sunday of December.

BEST TIME TO COME

Any time of the year is fine for a visit to the plantation; however, you may want to take in a festival so you'll want your trip to coincide with those dates in April, July, and December. Wildflowers in the spring bring many travelers to the area.

ADVENTURES IN LODGING AND DINING

Oak Shadows Cottage is a new guesthouse twenty miles south of Hempstead. After visiting the plantation, plan a trip to Liendo's Restaurant. The restaurant is owned by the plantation's current owners. Lunch is served seven days a week and dinner is available Friday and Saturday from 6:00 P.M. to 9:00 P.M. Groups of more than twelve should call ahead. Menus and prices are available online at www .liendo.org/restaurant.html.

FOR MORE INFORMATION

Contact Liendo Plantation online at www.liendo.org. The City of Hempstead Quarterly Newsletter is online at http://rtis.com/reg/ hempstead. For those who want to learn more about Elisabet Ney, a trip to Austin to visit her studio, now a museum, is in order. The Elisabet Ney Museum can be contacted at www.ci.austin.tx.us/elisabetney/. The museum is Ney's former art studio and portrait collection, and is one of the oldest museums in Texas.

Liendo Plantation, Hempstead. Vikk Simmons

NINE FLAGS OVER NACOGDOCHES, THE OLDEST TOWN IN TEXAS

NACOGDOCHES, TEXAS

Nacogdoches, the oldest town in Texas, is nestled deep in the woodlands of East Texas and is home to Stephen F. Austin University. Named for the Caddo family of Indians who once lived in that area, Nacogdoches has a twin city—Natchitoches in Louisiana. Among the many legends in Texas, one tells of a Caddo chief who had twin sons. Determined that his sons should become leaders of their own tribes, the chief sent them off for three days in different directions. One went toward the rising sun, the other toward the setting sun. The twin who went west settled in Nacogdoches; the twin who went toward the rising sun, made his home in Natchitoches, Louisiana.

From the time Spain established a mission in 1716, Nacogdoches was no longer a Caddo Indian settlement. Spanish trader Antonio Gil Y'Barbo became the leader of the settlers and received a grant from Mexico making Nacogdoches the first town in Texas. Over the next four decades, Nacogdoches played a vital role in Texas history. Welcome to the town in Texas that's flown nine flags.

ADVENTURES IN HISTORY

Many states never had their own flag, but six flags have flown over Texas. For the oldest town in Texas, Nacogdoches, that's still three fewer than they can claim. Although the French never settled in East Texas, the French flag flew over Nacogdoches from 1685 to 1689. Their many forays into this area forced the Spanish to establish permanent settlements in the small town. La Salle and his men, on their ill-fated journey to reach Mississippi, are said to have come through this East Texas area. In 1721 Spain grew tired of the French incursions into the region and established six missions and two presidios in East Texas. One of the missions was located in the area of present day Nacogdoches. Nacogdoches then lived under the Spanish flag. Most of the Spanish inhabitants left for San Antonio in 1763, but floods and an Indian raid there convinced three hundred survivors to return to Nacogdoches. They formed a Spanish town with two squares, one for government and the other for church. The government square, including a stone house, later known as the Old Stone Fort, was the official gateway to the Spanish district of Nacogdoches. The Old Stone Fort acted as headquarters for several of the unsuccessful attempts to establish Texas as a republic.

In 1812, Augustus Magee, a former officer in the U.S. Army, joined with Barnardo Gutierrez, and the two tried to take Texas. The Magee–Gutierrez flag replaced the earlier ones. Although they fought some major battles with Mexican forces, they were eventually defeated, and Texas was declared a province of Mexico. Then in 1819, along came Dr. James Long of Natchez, Mississippi, who mounted an expedition to claim Texas for the United States. He hoisted his own flag over Nacogdoches. Unfortunately, while trying to obtain the assistance of Jean Lafitte, the famous pirate and privateer, Long's group was wiped out. Although Long made a second attempt to claim Texas for the United States, he remained unsuccessful.

The Mexican flag was the next to fly over the Old Stone Fort. During the years 1821 to 1836, Nacogdoches grew, and its character changed, due in large part to the immigration from the southern United States. Anglo culture had arrived in Nacogdoches. Although remaining in the Mexican Confederation, Texas and Coahuila now formed one state. When Mexico gave Haden Edwards a contract to settle eight hundred families in Nacogdoches, he didn't expect to find all the land already settled by Indians and Mexican descendants. A dispute followed, and the Fredonia Rebellion began. Commanded by Edwards, this third attempt was made to free Texas from Mexico, which led to the flag of the Fredonia Rebellion flying atop the fort. Edwards led his men to the Old Stone Fort and named his followers Fredonians or freedom seekers. Even though the rebellion failed, the idea of colonizing Texas appealed to many Anglos. Mexico, seeing this, reversed its position on immigration and barred further entry.

What many call the opening gun of the Texas Revolution took place in August of 1832. In the Battle of Nacogdoches, five hundred citizens fought and drove the Mexican soldiers from the Stone Fort, pushing them back to the Angelina River before they finally surrendered. On March 2, 1836, Texas declared its independence from Mexico, and the Lone Star flag flew over the town. The Battle of Nacogdoches freed all areas east and north of San Antonio.

Although the residents had won freedom for their town, they continued to fight for Texas's freedom. After the revolution, the Confederate Stars and Bars also flew over the fort. Nacogdoches prospered its people raising cotton and tobacco and producing timber. The town retained its status as a cultural, educational, and religious center.

On October 13, 1845, Texas voters approved a U.S. annexation proposal. Two months later, Texas became the twenty-eighth state when

President James K. Polk signed the joint resolution for the admission of the State of Texas into the Union. By the time Texas joined the United States, eight flags had waved over Nacogdoches. Now the Stars and Stripes of the United States would be the ninth and the last to fly over a city that is often referred to as the cradle of Texas liberty. So, although the state claims six flags, Nacogdoches rightly holds the bragging rights to those six, plus those belonging to the three unsuccessful republics.

On the Map

Nacogdoches is approximately 135 miles from Houston and located at the intersections of U.S. Highway 59, State Highway 21, and State Highway 7. The town is also 65 miles south of Interstate 20.

Weekend Adventures

Walking through Millard's Crossing Historic Village with its collection of restored nineteenth-century buildings is like taking a walk into the past. Historic places such as Stone Fort Museum fill the town. If you like architecture and like to drive around town, then the Diedrich Rulfs Architectural Driving Tour with more than fifty homes, churches, and buildings would interest you. Four signers of the Texas Declaration of Independence are buried in Oak Grove Cemetery. The Old Nacogdoches University Building, built in 1859, originally housed the Nacogdoches University and later served as a hospital during the Civil War. Bibliophiles will love the Sterne-Hoya Library and Museum where the 3,000 books include a Texana collection. The Sterne-Hoya House, built in 1830 and said to be the oldest house in town, is filled with memorabilia from the early pioneer days of Texas. In 1902 the Old Stone Fort was torn down, but in 1936 some of the same stones were used to build the new replica of Old Stone Fort, now a museum.

Best Time to Visit

For a celebration of the town's history, time your visit with the annual Nine Flags Festival that runs from the Saturday before Thanksgiving through the second week in December. Labor Day weekend always draws a crowd to the annual Americana Music Festival. To add outdoor activities such as fishing, camping, and boating to your historical tour, spring and summer are the best choices. The Nacogdoches Azalea Trails are from the last two weeks of March through the first week in April, while the annual Texas Blueberry Festival is held the second week of June. Nacogdoches County is the state's number one producer of blueberries; visitors can enjoy blueberry farm tours.

Adventures in Lodging and Dining

The Fredonia Hotel, built by citizens for their guests and visitors, is located on Old Washington Square in the center of historic Nacogdoches. Over 350 years old, the hotel claims, "We have known Nine Flags in our 350 years" and invites visitors to "walk the red brick streets, explore centuries of Texas History and visit prehistoric Indian mounds, ancient cemeteries, and other historic sites all within walking distance of the hotel."

Constructed in 1892, the Hardeman Guest House welcomes guests today with all the amenities of the times. Historic bed and breakfasts include Brooks Cypress House, surrounded by nature and pine trees, and the Llano Grande Plantation, a 600-acre working tree farm in the Piney Woods. The John M. Sparks House and the Rosewild Home are both listed as Texas Historic Landmarks, while the Tol Barret House, listed on the National Register of Historic Places, is also a Texas State Landmark. All have been restored by hand and featured in several national magazines. Others include the Jones House, located in historic downtown Nacogdoches, and the Stepan Inn Guest Suites in Washington Square.

With plenty of dining available, visitors won't go hungry. Restaurants include Grannie's Kitchen; Clear Springs Restaurant, known for their grilled catfish and large stack of onion rings; and Yakofritz's Sandwich Shoppe, which has delectable homemade soups. For a relaxed evening of good dining, try D Gars's Bistro within walking distance of the Fredonia Hotel. Others include Butcher Boy's, Delacroix's Cajun Style Seafood, La Carreta, Dyes Kountry Katfish, and Szechuan's.

For More Information

If you'd like more information about this historical town, visit the website at www.visitnacogdoches.com or the Visitor's Center's site at www.ci.nacogdoches.tx.us/.

All Aboard!

──────── Palestine, Texas ────────

Palestine takes its name from Palestine, Illinois, the hometown of one of the earliest settlers to the area, Daniel Parker. The town was established in 1846, with the first courthouse built soon after and located on the crest of a low hill. Very quickly, small businesses opened around town, and paddle-wheel steamers helped commerce during periods of high water as they plied the Trinity River to Magnolia, the port for Palestine. However, the steamers lost the job when, in 1872, the International–Great Northern Railroad opened year-round travel to the east, to Houston and to Laredo.

Lots of cotton, lumber, cottonseed oil, and fruit were shipped from Palestine, and business boomed as a new district formed by the tracks resulted in two business areas, Old Town and New Town. The designations are still kept even though the two sections have long since grown together. When oil was found in 1928 at Boggy Creek, the town's economy diversified even further. This discovery saved Palestine, and unlike many towns, oil carried it through the Great Depression.

Today, Palestine has many different businesses including a beef-packing plant, various small establishments, and the railroad. It is also the

*Ticket window at the Palestine train depot. Elaine
L. Galit*

site of the National Scientific Balloon Facility, an operation of the National Aeronautics and Space Administration (NASA). Come spring, the
city plays host to thousands who visit the annual Texas Dogwood Trails.
Palestine is one of the terminals of the Texas State Railroad, now a state
park, that operates steam excursion trains between there and Rusk. As
such, it has added another dimension to its business base—tourism.

ADVENTURES IN HISTORY

Do you hear that whistle down the line? No, it's not the Chattanooga
Choo Choo calling you home; it's the Palestine/Rusk locomotive
hurtling through the Piney Woods of East Texas. And she does blow that
whistle loudly many times between Rusk and Palestine. In March or
April, look from the train windows and watch the white dogwood petals

drifting like snowflakes into the surrounding greenery. Eyes closed, bump along the 25 miles of track and over the Neches River on the longest of the twenty or so bridges you'll ride over. Listen to the clickity-clack as the rhythm mentally moves you back in time to the late 1800s, and the piercing whistle sounds its mournful call. Although the one-way trip takes about an hour and a half, don't leave your eyes closed too long. Instead, grab that camera and click away through the open window as the breeze blows through. If you're lucky, you might even spot a deer or a fox lurking in the underbrush.

Although not the original depots at Rusk or Palestine, the current buildings are authentic and are constructed of native materials. They are also unique and have been used in many movies and TV commercials. The trains leave both depots as the same time, so you can board in either Rusk or Palestine. Be sure to wave to the other passengers as the trains meet each other at the midway mark at Mewshaw Siding.

ON THE MAP

Palestine, Texas, the county seat of Anderson County, is located at the intersection of U.S. Highways 79 and 287, at the center of the county, some 108 miles southeast of Dallas and 150 miles north of Houston.

WEEKEND ADVENTURES

For a taste of Palestine history, make your way to the Museum for East Texas Culture, located in the old Palestine High School building built in 1915–1916. Scheduled for demolition in 1976, the building was saved when a group of citizens decided to restore it and open a museum. The museum opened in 1982 and contains displays and exhibits from art to business machines, and a large collection of business and commercial historical documents and genealogical records. More records can be found at the City of Palestine Library and the Anderson County Historic Commission.

To visit the early pioneer days in Palestine, go to the Howard House Museum built in 1851. Although you must call ahead to pre-arrange a visit, the National Scientific Balloon Facility is a exceptional place to see. Of course, no trip to Palestine would be complete without the train ride to Rusk on the Texas State Railroad. No time for the trip? Visit the park.

BEST TIME TO VISIT

March and April promise beautiful weather for a train ride. Held annually the last two weekends in March and the first weekend in April, the Texas Dogwood Trails Celebration offers three weekends of events revolving around the beauty and mystery of the dogwood tree. The dogwood trees are in bloom, and the town is awash in the purple splendor of wisteria trees. However, with an average temperature of 71 degrees, it's no wonder the Chamber of Commerce notes that "Dogwoods, Azaleas, Fall colors, Spring flowers, any season is a good reason to visit Palestine."

ADVENTURES IN LODGING AND DINING

Palestine's bed and breakfasts combine history with quaint charm. For a park-like atmosphere complete with gardens and a porch swing, head out to Apple Annie's Bed and Breakfast. Other bed and breakfast options include Fox Meadows, with its acres of forests and pasture land, and the rural, rustic ranchhouse setting of Bailey's Bunkhouse, as well as the Bar-S Ranch, Bowers Mansion, Dyerwood, and the restored plantation called Bed and Breakfast at Tiffany's.

For a cattleman's dinner, try the Ranch House in Old Town Palestine. Other restaurants include Giovanni's Italian Restaurant on West Oak and the Coffee Landing Restaurant on Lake Palestine.

FOR MORE INFORMATION

Maps and self-guided tours are found at the Visitor's Center (www.visit palestine.com). Online, check the Palestine Area Chamber of Commerce's website www.palestine-online.org. Information about the Texas State Railroad is available at 800-442-8951 or 903-683-2561. Texas Dogwood Trails information is available at 800-659-3484.

A GHOST TOWN BUILDS A THRIVING CITY

RUSK, TEXAS

Trains, tracks, and oil wells helped the town of Rusk become a city. When Thomas J. Rusk came to Texas in 1834, he was looking for his business partners who had embezzled his company's funds. Unfortunately, he was never able to regain his investment, but he liked what he saw in Rusk and stayed, even joining in the revolution. Not only did he fight at San Jacinto, he also signed the Texas Declaration of Indepen-

Railway Station in Rusk. Elaine L. Galit

dence and became secretary of war for a brief time under President Sam Houston; he and Houston were the first senators to the United States Congress from Texas. Little wonder that in 1995 the Texas Historical Commission designated Rusk as an official Texas Main Street city. Rusk is also the birthplace of Texas's first native-born governor James Stephen Hogg. His residence, called Mountain Home at that time, is now known as Jim Hogg State Park and is a popular tourist site.

The Texas State Railroad was actually built to serve the Rusk unit of the Texas State Prison System, a far cry from the popular tourist attraction it's become today. The foundry at the penitentiary developed the Texas iron ore industry and eventually caused the beginning of the city of New Birmingham. Today oil wells dot Rusk, a thriving city and a commercial center for agriculture, lumber, and iron ore. The town attracts many tourists with the natural beauty of Rusk State Park and the fun of the Texas State Railroad trip to neighboring Palestine.

ADVENTURES IN HISTORY

Although Rusk is thriving today, its history is tied in with a ghost town. The town didn't start out haunted, of course. New Birmingham was supposed to rival its two namesakes in Alabama and England. A sewing machine salesman, Anderson Blevins, had an ambitious dream. He found iron ore in Cherokee County and decided that since the ore was already mined to supply Rusk Penitentiary, why not lease some acres and start a big mining company. With the help of some capitalists, he built a 50-ton furnace that Blevins named Tassie Belle after his wife. Before long a town sprang up with a bank, saloons, a newspaper, and even a hotel. Industries thrived and New Birmingham seemed to be on the same path as the other Birminghams.

But times dealt the dreamers a severe blow in 1893 when the Panic of 1893 caused capital to dry up. More trouble struck when one of the town's businessmen killed W. H. Hammons, one of the capitalists who started with Blevins, and a fire destroyed the furnace causing many employees to be laid off. People moved, businesses closed, and the city faded into oblivion.

During the First World War, Rusk needed materials for construction. The New Birmingham buildings were available, and materials from these were used to further the development of structures in Rusk. Sadly, the last New Birmingham building left standing, the hotel, burned to the ground, and even its debris was finally removed. Aside from a large granite monument in front of the Texas Highway Department and a small walking trail on the west side of the highway, all that remained of Blevins's dream was in the memories of those who had dwelled in the short-lived town—the once promising city of New Birmingham.

On the Map

Rusk, Texas, is located near the geographic center of the county at the junction of U.S. Highways 69 and 84 and State Highway 110 where they link up with many farm roads.

Weekend Adventures

From mid-March through October, enjoy history as the Iron Horse travels from Rusk to Palestine and back. For outdoor fun at its best, wander over next to the railroad park and camp in the hundred-acre pine tree–filled area of Rusk State Park. The park has a 15-acre lake and comes complete with camping facilities. Other attractions include the Jim Hogg City Historical Park. Boasting itself as the home of the first native-born governor of Texas, the town invites visitors to view the Mountain Home Museum. Take a walk along the 546-foot footbridge, built in 1861 and said to be the nation's longest bridge, aptly named Footbridge Park.

Those who love historic architecture will want to visit the first bank in Cherokee County, the 1865 Bonner Bank building, and the Cherokee Theater, a restored movie house downtown. Another site to see is the Old Rusk Penitentiary Building where the prisoners fabricated the dome of the state capitol and other iron structures.

The Old Bonner Bank in Rusk still stands. Elaine L. Galit

BEST TIME TO VISIT

On the fourth Saturday in May, Rusk holds both its Fair on the Square and the Annual Street Dance. Another good time to visit is on the second Saturday in October when the Pioneer Festival coincides with the Indian Summer Arts and Crafts Fair.

ADVENTURES IN LODGING AND DINING

Although there is plenty of conventional lodging in Rusk, the town has some special places. Voted Best Weekend Getaway by Inn-goers and *Arrington's Inn Traveler's 2004 Book of Lists*, Almost HeavInn Bed & Breakfast in Rusk is just that. From the peaceful country surroundings of the thirty-five acres of wooded rolling hills, gardens, and a lake, to the home-baked biscuits and muffins, this is a place to enjoy your end-of-day leisure.

Not far down the road, Fox Meadows in Palestine invites the weary visitor with the slogan "Let the stars be your nightlight and the birds be your wake-up call." Another place to rest, also not far away, is Lake Palestine Bed & Breakfast in Frankston, Texas. This New Orleans–style lakeside inn is located on the shores of Lake Palestine near Tyler.

Although many like to picnic in the flower-laden parks, there are also ample dining facilities in town. Aside from the fast-food chains, try Bodacious Bar-B-Que, the Pitt Grill, or Beverly's Country Café. According to Bob Bowman in *The East Texas Sunday Drive Book*, Dot's Cafe, located on Martin Luther King Street in Rusk, has the best soul food in East Texas, and the Thomas J. Rusk Hotel dining room offers items that range from Cornish hen to bread pudding.

The "Welcome to Rusk" sign greets train passengers. Elaine L. Galit

For More Information

To gather more information about Rusk, check out the Chamber of Commerce website at www.rusktx.com. To learn more about the Rusk/Palestine train trip, go to www.texasstaterailroad.com.

Living Large with the Stark Family

—— Stark Civic Plaza, Orange, Texas ——

The city of Orange, Texas, is forever linked with Texas independence because they both came into existence during the same year. However, that was not the beginning of Orange. The town had sported a number of names before it evolved into Orange. The high banks on the Sabine River lured many early pioneers to the area then known as "Green's Bluff." Other names included Huntley, Lower Town of Jefferson, and Madison, but the emergence of the town of Madisonville made the residents decide to make one more name change. One story says it comes from the home of an early surveyor, Orange, New Jersey; another suggests the name comes from the native orange groves lining the riverbanks.

As most places in Texas, Orange had its share of hardships and heartaches. Storms, wars, and lawlessness mark the town's history. Orange historian H. C. Williams remarks that in 1879 the local superintendent reported that the city had earned a reputation of being a rowdy and lawless industrial town. The superintendent sought the help of the Rev. Vital Quinon, a native of France known as "the fighting priest" for his earlier effective work battling the outbreak of ruffians in Denison, Texas. History shows that the priest proved to be the right man for the job.

Major changes occurred in 1914 when the harbor was dredged. The city prospered until the Depression Era; however, World War II marked the end of hard times. The city's population grew from 7,000 to 60,000 nearly overnight with the installation of a U.S. Naval Station. But during the course of its history, one family influenced the beauty that the city exhibits even today: the Starks and their descendants, the Lutchers, and the Browns.

ADVENTURES IN HISTORY

While the early history of Orange may have been wild and woolly, the city achieved a breadth of Victorian beauty and elegance through the Stark family's ability to live large and give grand. The family traveled the world and brought to this southeast Texas town breathtaking art and architecture. This is a family who knew how to enjoy wealth, but they also knew that great riches bring even greater responsibility. Their legacy stands in the center of Orange as a testament to their philanthropy and a reminder to others of how great an impact one family can have on a town. Orange is richer because of their existence and their gifts.

If you take a walk through downtown Orange, you'll come upon a three-block area known as the Stark Civic Plaza. If there is one thing the Starks knew, it was how to be bigger-than-life philanthropists. The Stark House and the Lutcher Memorial Building are on the National Register of Historical Places.

The First Presbyterian Church and Lutcher Memorial Building (http://208.17.151.189/fpo/), built by Frances Ann Lutcher as a memorial to her husband, Henry Jacob Lutcher, is an architectural wonder. Although dedicated in 1912, the planning for the church began in 1893 at the Chicago Worlds Fair when Frances Lutcher saw three leaded stained-glass windows of immense proportion crafted by the renowned J & R Lamb Studios of New York. The church has a distinctive dome of 36-foot diameter opalescent glass. The exterior is made of the same Texas pink granite that is used on the State Capitol in Austin. There are thirty-one leaded stained-glass windows in the entranceway, sanctuary, and Fellowship Hall. Visitors sit in awe at the sight of the wonderful combination of art and architecture.

The W. H. Stark House (www.whstarkhouse.org), a restored 1894 Victorian home that belonged to William H. and Miriam Lutcher, con-

tains more than 7,000 artifacts that once belonged to the family. The tour includes the carriage house and the three-story, fifteen-room home. The house is a Recorded Texas Historic Landmark.

The Stark Museum (www.starkmuseum.org) is a delight. Of particular interest are what the museum describes as double-elephant-size folios of John J. Audubon's *Birds of America*. The museum contains Native American artifacts, art of the American West, and much more. Lutcher Stark's collection of early Taos Society artists is what the curator calls one of the largest collections of Southwest art in the United States.

The Frances Ann Lutcher Theater for Performing Arts (www.lutcher .org) achieved status as one of the ten largest nonprofit performing-arts series in Texas. This is a one thousand–seat theater where musicals, concerts, opera, and drama are performed

On the Map

Orange is located on Interstate 10 in the corner of Southeast Texas on the western bank of the Sabine River and is about one hundred miles east of Houston. The river divides Texas and Louisiana.

Weekend Adventures

The Heritage House Museum, a large, two-story building built in 1902, is listed in the National Register of Historic Places and is designated a Recorded Texas Historic Landmark. The central fire station has an antique fire engine and fire-fighting memorabilia on display. There are plenty of other attractions in southeast Texas to fill a traveler's schedule for a day, a week, or even a month. Don't miss the 250-acre reserve Shangri La Botanical Gardens and Nature Center, initiated by H. J. Lutcher Stark in 1942. Super Gator Tours offers tours of alligator-filled swamps that are popular with plant and bird lovers as well. Orange's general store, the Farmers Mercantile, on W. Division dates back to 1928 and has a wide range of items for the shopping addict. A trip to Piney

Woods Country Winery can test the weary traveler's taste buds with fruit wines made of blackberry, plum, peach, and even pecan mocha. Call for an appointment. Orange is also a stop on the Great Texas Coastal Birding Trail.

Best Time to Visit

While Texas is hot in the summer, the Stark Civic Plaza buildings, including the church, are air conditioned, so the heat won't interfere with your visit.

Adventures in Lodging and Dining

The Rogers House and Caroline's Bed and Breakfast are located in the historical district. Campgrounds are also available. Orange has a number of restaurants but one in particular has a unique setting: the Old Orange Café on Division Street, within walking distance of downtown attractions, offers daily specials and homemade desserts and is set in a renovated dairy.

For More Information

For more historical information on Orange, Texas, go to the website maintained by historian and author Howard C. Williams (www .hcwilliams.com). The city maintains a website at www.orangetexas.net. Visitors will find helpful information such as maps and hotel and restaurant suggestions as well as a list of Texas Historical Markers for the area. The Greater Orange Area Chamber of Commerce's website is www.goacc.org. A resourceful Web page for the southeast Texas area is Fun in Southeast Texas (www.fun365days.com). The website is a tourism page sponsored by the Partnership of Southeast Texas that includes nine Southeast Texas counties. For more information on the Stark Foundation, go to www.starkfoundation.org.

Eighteen Minutes That Changed Texas History

San Jacinto Battleground
State Historical Park

So sudden and fierce was the enemy's charge that the earth seemed to move and tremble.

—*General Antonio Lopez de Santa Anna, April 22, 1836*

Every year hundreds of reenactors gather for a mock battle to celebrate the Battle of San Jacinto. San Jacinto Volunteers, Daughters of the Republic, San Jacinto Museum of History Association, and the Texas Parks and Wildlife Department come together to make the event meaningful and accurate. Families, schoolchildren, and history buffs join in as spectators while muskets fire, cannons boom, and actors yell. At the end of the battle the tradition still holds of the Texas Army Fife and Drum Corps' rendition of the song Texians played on the battlefield in 1836, "Will You Come to the Bower?"

The San Jacinto Battleground State Historic Site preserves the history and the memory of that fateful day. The site is a National Historic Landmark. The complex consists of the battleground, monument, and the battleship *Texas.*

Adventures in History

After the fateful events that occurred during the Fall of the Alamo, followed by the massacre at Goliad, the Texan army had little hope. In fact, the army was losing men in what was later to be called the Runaway Scrape. The Mexican army was advancing, the Texan army was retreating, and the men feared for their families. Many left to help their loved ones in the face of Santa Anna's advance.

In spite of the troubles, Sam Houston pressed on toward the Sabine. Houston pushed to follow Santa Anna and his army to Buffalo Bayou, then on to Lynch's Ferry. On April 20 a high-pitched skirmish occurred between General Sherman and the Mexican army. The next morning, Houston ordered Deaf Smith to destroy Vince's Bridge. This not only prevented any further increase to the Mexican Army ranks but also sealed the fate of his forces and Santa Anna's. There was no turning back.

At 3:30 in the afternoon, siesta time, on April 21, 1836, Santa Anna's army slept. The Texan army numbered 750 to Santa Anna's 1,500. In spite of the odds, Houston slipped his men into position behind the trees. The "Twin Sisters" cannon in place, Houston and his men moved forward.

All at once, with cries of "Remember the Alamo," "Remember Bahia," and "Remember Goliad," Houston's army attacked. The Mexican army never stood a chance. The Mexican army's losses were staggering: 630 dead and 730 taken prisoner. Amazingly, Houston's army suffered 9 dead or mortally wounded and 30 wounded. The entire battle took eighteen minutes.

Less than a month later, the Treaty of Velasco was signed. Although the war was declared officially over, neither government truly accepted the declaration.

Today the San Jacinto monument commemorates April 21, 1836, with the following words: "Measured by its results, San Jacinto was one of the most decisive battles of the world. The freedom of Texas from Mexico won here led to annexation and to the Mexican War, resulting in the acquisition by the United States of the States of Texas, New Mexico, Arizona, Nevada, California, Utah, and parts of Colorado, Wyoming, Kansas and Oklahoma. Almost one-third of the present area of the American nation, nearly a million square miles of territory, changed sovereignty."

On the Map

The complex is located 22 miles east of Houston and a short distance from Galveston and is on State Highway 134 at San Jacinto Battle-grounds State Historic Site in La Porte, southeast of Houston.

Weekend Adventures

The monument is dedicated to the "Heroes of the Battle of San Jacinto and to all others who contributed to the independence of Texas." A 34-foot star representing the Lone Star Republic tops the 570-foot shaft. It is the tallest stone column memorial structure in the world and weighs 70,300,000 pounds. Make sure you ride to the top to the observation floor. The San Jacinto Museum of History houses more than four hundred years of Texas history. The battleship *Texas* is the first battleship memorial museum in the United States. The *Texas* is the last battleship patterned after HMS *Dreadnought* and she was launched March 12, 1914. The *Texas* is both a National Historic Landmark and a National Mechanical Engineering Landmark.

Best Time to Visit

If you want to see the mock battle, plan a visit around April 21. Contact the complex or the website for the actual date, as the event is scheduled for Saturdays.

Adventures in Lodging and Dining

Overnight accommodations can be found in Houston, LaPorte, and Galveston, all within easy distance from the complex. Many visitors plan to picnic at the park. Picnic tables, grills, and water faucets are available in the recreation area. The Ship's Galley, a snack shop with a limited menu, is next to the battleship *Texas*.

For More Information

For more information go to the website at www.tpwd.state.us/park/battlesh/.

THE MELTING POT OF TEXAS

———— VICTORIA, TEXAS ————

Founded in 1824 with only forty-one Mexican families, Victoria is the second oldest incorporated city in Texas and the county seat of Victoria County. The city was recognized early on as a town with many traditions such as farming and cattle ranching. Later, Victoria would become a player in the oil and gas industry, a venture that is vital to this day. Many of Victoria's business enterprises are quite unique, such as a safe and vault company and a company manufacturing the first oleomargarine and gelatin from animal fats, using the first refrigerator cars for transport. Along with cattle ranching and meatpacking, Victoria boasted three banks by 1900. Two are Texas's oldest banks.

Take a visit to the historic downtown and close your eyes. Listen to the squeak and moan of the wooden wheels as the wagons make their way through town. Or hear the "clip clop" of the mule-drawn streetcar with its four cars named for popular ladies in the city. Smell the green of the native grasses mingling with the odor of cattle. Hear the lowing sounds of those cattle calling through the breeze. Now, open your eyes to see some of Victoria's oldest buildings, including the original O'Connor-Proctor Building that eventually became the Victoria Bank and Trust. The oldest church in Victoria is Saint Mary's. Some homes have been well maintained to keep their imaginative charm and are still owned by descendants of the original owners. Now a far cry from the first forty-plus families, Victoria's more than 60,000 people extend an invitation to visit the city where yesterday and today mingle with tomorrow.

ADVENTURES IN HISTORY

What we now call Victoria, Texas, was actually established in 1824 by Martín De Léon as a Mexican town called Guadalupe Victoria. Originally known as Cypress Grove for the many cypress trees lining the banks of the Guadalupe River, the town later took its name from the first president

of the republic of Mexico. Although it remained a Mexican settlement, Guadalupe Victoria sent supplies and men to support the Texas Revolution in the form of the Victoria Militia, led by Placido Benavides, De Léon's son-in-law. After the Texas victory at San Jacinto, the Mexicans in town were ostracized and left Guadalupe Victoria. This left the town wide open for the Anglos to move in, and they promptly changed the name to Victoria. In 1839 the town incorporated under the Republic of Texas.

Victoria, like so many small settlements of that time, suffered from multiple setbacks. People were killed in the Comanche raid that destroyed Linnville. Others died during the terrible cholera epidemic. Two German immigrants, Dillman Mantz and his son, as well as a black man called Black Peter, struggled valiantly to arrange proper burials for the rapidly dying townspeople during the epidemic.

Even with all the hardships, the town continued to grow, as Indianola became a port of entry for many immigrants. The surge of refugees spilled over, and a large number settled in Victoria. Along with Americans, there were Germans, Irish, Lebanese, Bohemians, Italians, Jews from several different countries, Mexicans, and even Czechoslovakians. The population changed from purely Anglo, with one free black man, to a multi-ethnic mix, as families arrived with names such as Fritz, Mackay, Dupree, Levi, and O'Connor. The new settlers brought technological, economic, and social changes that caused a rapid alteration in the growth of Victoria as it shifted from rural to urban.

To savor Victoria's past, stroll under the twelve lamp posts in De Leon Plaza and Market Square. Each lamp has a bronze memorial plate saluting the city's diverse pioneers. Imitating a practice in Victoria, British Columbia, the folks of Victoria, Texas, place flowers below the light fixtures for all to enjoy.

On the Map

Victoria is located north of Corpus Christi in southeast Texas, about 80 miles southwest of Houston and 116 miles southeast of San Antonio.

Weekend Adventures

As one of the older towns in Texas, Victoria teems with historical sites. Travel down Highway 59 by the Guadalupe River to find the historical marker designating the probable location of the city's original site. Victoria's first public burial ground, Evergreen Cemetery, is located east of downtown. Years ago the town placed an inscribed commemorative stone, along with the original gatepost from the Welder Mansion, at the site. The bandstand in De Leon Plaza, rebuilt around 1895, stands on top of a foundation from the city's old standpipe water reservoir. With a natural background of green leaves and branches from an overhanging tree, the statue "Firing Line" graces the De Leon Plaza as the soldier's grip tightens on his rifle. Designed by noted sculptor Pompeo Coppini, the Confederate statue is intended to be a fitting tribute to the men who fought.

If Texana is your passion, check out the McNamara Historical Museum with its collection of documents and artifacts from Spanish, Mexican, and Texan historical times. Antique furnishings also embellish the museum located in an 1876 Victorian homestead.

Ever wondered what type of animal thrives in the Texas waterways—or met a living relic of the dinosaur age? A special place for visitors is the six-acre Texas Zoo. Named the National Zoo of Texas in 1984, the popular attraction is located in Riverside Park next to the Guadalupe River. Other interesting sights include the Riverside Park & Rose Garden, Victoria Botanical Gardens, Community Art Center, Victoria County Courthouse, and the Nave Museum, named for the Texas artist Royston Nave who painted in and around Victoria in the 1920s.

Best Time to Visit

Visit during the spring and enjoy the Victorian Ballet Theater's Spring Gala, or the Bach Festival held during the month of June. The Historic Home Tours are held in April.

Adventures in Lodging and Dining

Drive down the Street of Ten Friends district to the Friendly Oaks Bed and Breakfast, built in 1915, nestled among huge live oak trees. In this quiet historic residential area, breakfasts featuring Texas produce help the ambiance of this bed and breakfast with its historical themed rooms.

Victoria has a large array of restaurants guaranteed to please every palate. For fun and good food, visit the Rosebud Fountain and Grill named for Victoria's City of Roses designation in the 1920s–1940s. Along with its brightly colored chairs and music memorabilia, enjoy home-cooked food, like Mrs. Raby's crabmeat stuffed jalapenos, in a 1940s-era soda fountain setting.

For a change of pace, try red snapper cooked in banana leaves at the Taqueria Victoria or wander over to the Siesta Restaurant for some Mama's Nachos. Prefer fish? Head on out to Colet Inn Bar and Grill for catfish and friendly service in a country atmosphere. If hungry is your middle name, try Montana Mike's for a 44- or 66-oz. Steak, or the Feed-lot Steakhouse located at the Victoria Regional Airport.

For More Information

For travel information, try the Victoria Convention & Visitors Bureau website at www.victexchamber.org. Go online for information about the National Zoo of Texas at www.texaszoo.org/. Want to know about the festivals? Check online at www.victoriatexasinfo.com/links.html.

5

In and Around
San Antonio

Texas historian and journalist Frank Tolbert once said, "Every Texan has two homes, his own and San Antonio." San Antonio celebrates her rich cultural heritage every day and welcomes her fellow Texans and the world with open arms. For many Texans, the heart of their second home in San Antonio is the local shrine known as the Alamo. Long considered a mecca for many history buffs and now the ninth largest city in the nation, San Antonio is ranked as the number one destination in Texas by the Texas Historical Commission. Considering the reverence Texans hold for the site, the numbers should not be unexpected.

Visitors to the vibrant, colorful city will not be disappointed with the city of fiestas. Mention San Antonio, Texas, and for many the image of the famous Paseo del Rio or River Walk comes to mind. The annual Fiesta San Antonio Celebration draws 200,000-plus people simply for the river parade. More than 3,000,000 visitors and participants attend the annual commemoration of the Battle of Flowers. Since 1891, the Battle of the Flowers has honored the heroes of the Alamo and the Battle of San Jacinto. The Fiesta San Antonio Commission (www.fiesta-sa.org) recalls the early commemoration day battles when women, after decorating the horse-drawn carriages, would parade in front of the Alamo and throw flowers at one another.

Built in 1731, the San Fernando Cathedral has been at the heart of San Antonio for centuries, and today more than five thousand attend weekend Mass. For many Texans, a trip to San Antonio is incomplete without a visit to the San Antonio Missions National Historic Park. The four Spanish frontier missions preserved are Missions San Jose, San Juan, Espada, and Concepcion. More than 1,300,000 people visited the park in 2003. Most start at Mission San Jose.

ADVENTURES IN HISTORY

The San Antonio River is dotted with the remains of Spanish missions built in the 1700s. Established by Franciscan friars, the missions may be dedicated to God and worship, but visitors would be mistaken if they thought that was all they were. The Franciscans, under a royal decree, accompanied the conquering Spanish army and helped establish what were essentially outposts of the Spanish empire in America. Founded in 1720, Mission San Jose, the Queen of the Missions, was the largest of those on the San Antonio River. The mission is often mistaken for a fort, but that is okay. Built for protection, the walls around the compound were intended to discourage Apache attacks. Rumors of underground tunnels connecting the missions have been around for years but never proven.

A legend grew up around the Rose Window, La Ventana de Rosa, the south window of the sacristy. Pedro Huizar, the sculptor, carved the window in 1775. One story suggests that he carved the window for his beloved, Rosa, who still lived in Spain. When he finished the work, he sent for her. When she died in a shipwreck, he became grief-stricken and adopted a vow of celibacy. He spent the rest of his life carving the church's limestone façade. However, San Antonio has a number of families who claim descent from the famous sculptor and dispute the story. Another version suggests that a stonemason, working on the mission, fell in love with a local woman. When the she fell ill and died, the stonemason built the rose window to her memory. Some folks even swear they've seen the woman in the window.

Today, the mission shows the wear and tear of weather, time, and man. In 1850 the U.S. Army used the carvings for target practice, but fortunately the restoration has succeeded in preserving the façade for today's visitors.

On the Map

Sometimes called the gateway to southern Texas, San Antonio sits in the middle of the lower half of the state, about 80 miles from Austin and 200 miles from Dallas and from Houston. The San Antonio Missions National Historical Park is located along the San Antonio River from Mission Concepcion on the north to Mission Espada on the south. The marked trail runs between the various sites. Travelers often begin their trip along the mission trail with a visit to the first mission, the Alamo.

Weekend Adventures

There are too many historical sites to list, but one you won't want to miss is Fort Sam, located northeast of downtown. A former training site for many of the Buffalo Soldiers, the fort contains the Fort Sam Houston Museum and the U.S. Army Medical Department Museum. The Casa Navarro State Historic Site, once the home of Texas hero Jose Navarro, is the only historic site in San Antonio dedicated to interpreting Mexican history and the heritage of Texas, done through the life of the San Antonio merchant, rancher, and statesman. Located on the left bank of the San Antonio River, you'll find La Villita, the city's first settlement that was comprised of Spanish soldiers stationed at the Mission San Antonio de Valero, commonly known as the Alamo. Today La Villita is an active arts community with historic charm and small restaurants. The Steves Homestead is a mansion in the Historic King William District. Looking for a great view of the city? Go to the Tower of the

America's observation deck or hop onto one of the San Antonio street-cars to take in one or more of the five historic districts downtown.

BEST TIME TO VISIT

The San Antonio Living History Organization (www.sanantonioliving history.com) commemorates the sacrifices made by the heroes of the Alamo with annual Dawn at the Alamo and Remember the Alamo events. Fiesta San Antonio (www.fiesta-sa.org) is a ten-day citywide event in the spring, and Cinco de Mayo commemorates the Mexican Army's defeat of the French at the Battle of Puebla on May 5, 1862. The Texas Folklife Festival occurs in June and features many different Texas cultures. Another favorite is the Holiday River Parade and Lighting Ceremony in December. If you plan a mid-February visit, check out the San Antonio Livestock Show and Rodeo.

ADVENTURES IN LODGING AND DINING

San Antonio's historic German district, King William Street, is a bed and breakfast lover's dream and provides an architectural excursion into the Texas past. The historic Menger Hotel is full of grand stories about Teddy Roosevelt and is said to have had its share of ghostly visitors. Built in the 1920s and fully renovated, the Emily Morgan Hotel sits next door to the Alamo. Riverwalk hotels include the Westin Riverwalk and Inn on the River. The Jackson House, one of two Noble Inns in the King William Historic District, is the only bed and breakfast to receive both a Four Diamond rating from AAA and a Mobile Travel Guide Three Star rating.

A visit to HemisFair Park, the site of the 1968 World's Fair and home of the Tower of the Americas as well as the location of the Institute of Texan Cultures and Mexican Cultures, also provides a variety of restaurants. Dining along the riverwalk is a dream experience, with many restaurants ready to play their part. For a cowboy experience, the Diamond W Longhorn Ranch tempts visitors with a chuck wagon supper, a

cowboy show, and an old general store. Sunset Station is in the 1902 Southern Pacific train station in the historic St. Paul Square District and offers plenty of shopping, dining, and entertainment.

For More Information

Contact the San Antonio Convention and Visitors Bureau for a complete listing of events and attractions (www.SanAntonioVisit.com). The Visitor Center is located at 317 Alamo Plaza.

The Cry of the Alamo Echoes across Time and Space

——— The Alamo, San Antonio, Texas ———

In the courtyard of the convent in the Alamo sits a small, granite monument that speaks of large deeds and even larger hopes. To many the Alamo site is hallowed ground. The heroes of the Alamo are linked with the heroes of the Battle of Nagashino in sixteenth-century Japan and the Chinese Battle of Suiyang in the eighth century. Across the world and through the centuries, heroic deeds are remembered and the similarity of the deeds remarked upon.

Adventures in History

In 1914 a Japanese citizen and renowned scholar presented Texans with a monument commemorating the heroes of the Alamo and Japan. When Professor Shigetaka Shiga, a Waseda University professor in Tokyo, was a boy, he had read the story of the Battle of the Alamo and the heroism of the Alamo's defenders. He had also read of the famous Japanese Battle of Nagashino that took place near his birthplace centuries before and noted the similarities between the two battles. Each one claimed a hero who had sneaked through enemy lines to seek help, and who then returned to continue his participation in the battle. Dr. Shiga had an inscription put on the back of the monument, calling the Nagashino warrior Suneemon Torii the "Bonham of Japan." Both Bonham and Torii returned from their missions through enemy lines only to sacrifice their lives for their fellow defenders.

The heroic comparison went even further when Dr. Shiga had the poem linking the Battle of the Alamo with the eighth-century Chinese Battle of Suiyang inscribed on the front of the monument. The poem is written in Kanbun, a classical style of Chinese. The stone slab of granite rests on a base that is a stone from the battlefield site at Nagashino near the grave of Suneemon Torii. A similar monument was also erected at Okazaki, Japan. In this way Dr. Shiga felt he had extended the bridge between the East and the West in the actions of these heroic defenders. At the Alamo dedication ceremony, Dr. Shiga said, "I shall strive to make my people understand the friendliness, generosity, and hospitality of the inhabitants of far-off America."

On the Map

The Alamo is at 300 Alamo Plaza in San Antonio. Parking is available at several pay lots nearby. To reach the Alamo from U.S. 281/Interstate 37 southbound, exit at Houston Street, turn right and proceed three blocks to Avenue E, turn left and continue to the intersection of Houston and Alamo Plaza. From Interstate 37 northbound, exit at Commerce Street, turn left on Commerce and proceed 10 blocks to Alamo Plaza, turn right and continue for one and a half blocks. Admission is free. Hours are Monday through Friday, 9:00 A.M. until 5:30 P.M.; Saturday through Sunday, 10:00 A.M. until 5:30 P.M.

——— Weekend Adventures ———

The Alamo is ranked the top attraction in Texas. According to Richard Bruce Winders, Ph.D., Historian and Curator of the Alamo, visitors have a deeper appreciation and a better experience if they realize that despite the modern serene setting, the grounds were the stage for a fierce battle. Remnants of the original structure can be found throughout the compound. There are two walking tours: the Alamo Walking Tour and the Battlefield Walking Tour. Although there are five gates that access the compound, many prefer to enter the old church or modern shrine, where visitors find artifacts relating to the Alamo heroes, such as Davy Crockett's buckskin vest. This building was also the scene of the fiercest fighting during the 1836 battle. A visit to Alamo Gardens and the Wall of History is for those truly interested in the Alamo's 300-year history. The Barrack Museum and a viewing of the 17-minute film on the Alamo produced by the History Channel are two more items of interest, and don't forget the cannons in the Cavalry Courtyard and the massive live oak tree in Covento Courtyard. Around the plaza are commemorating plaques and original foundation stones that date back to the original Alamo of 1836.

Downtown San Antonio is full of wonderful places and opportunities. Stroll from Paseo del Alamo to Paseo del Rio or River Walk and take in La Villita, the restored "Little Village," or ride on the old-time streetcars. Visit the Menger Hotel where Teddy Roosevelt stayed long ago, or stop by the Hertzberg Circus Museum.

Best Time to Visit

While any time is a good time to visit the Alamo, you may want to have your visit coincide with special activities going on in San Antonio such as the Fiestas Patrias or occur in the spring when the Texas landscape is full of wildflowers. San Antonio is a festival city, so there are plenty of times throughout the year to match a visit with a big celebration. Just remember, summer in Texas is hot.

Adventures in Lodging and Dining

For a true historical treat, try the Beckman Inn and Carriage House Bed and Breakfast, a historic landmark downtown across from the Riverwalk and in the King William Historic District. The inn is listed in the National Register of Historic Places. From the Alamo, take the trolley for about a five-minute ride to the historical district. Another famous historical lodging is the Menger Hotel where you can sleep steeped in history and picture Teddy Roosevelt at the hotel bar. Any visit to San Antonio must include a trip to the river, and there you'll find restaurants offering a multicultural dining experience such as Cajun, Mexican, French, German, Spanish, Tex-Mex, and even good old American style.

For More Information

The Alamo is operated by the Daughters of the Republic of Texas. For information call 210-225-1391 or check the website www.thealamo.org. Be sure and check with the San Antonio Visitors and Convention Bureau and order their tourist package at 1-800-531-5700 or visit their website at www.sanantoniocvb.com.

Why Farm Boys Became Cowboys

——— Bandera, Texas ———

Welcome to Bandera, the Cowboy Capital of the World!

Bandera is located northwest of San Antonio and south of Kerrville, in the beautiful hill country of West Texas. This small town projects a large vision of the Old West, one that includes a riot of flowers such as Indian paintbrush, yellow coreopsis, Indian blankets, daisies, and of course, the legendary bluebonnet of Texas. The source of the town's name is a legend as well. Actually, there are two accounts. According to folklore, after the battles between Apache and Comanche Indians and the Spanish Conquistadors, a red "Abandera," Spanish for flag or banner, was flown to define the boundary between Spanish and Indian hunting grounds. The other possibility is that the town was named after a Spanish officer called Bandera.

Bandera has one of the oldest Polish communities in the United States. Sixteen Polish families settled in Bandera to run the mill that manufactured cypress shingles. The town shows off a great deal of Polish architecture including St. Stanislaus Catholic Church, the second oldest Polish church in America. A river town, Bandera has spent its history cozying up to the Medina River and her cypress-lined beds. After 1900, a series of floods devastated the economy, and Bandera remained pretty much inaccessible until 1936 when the San Antonio highway was built.

Incorporated in 1964, Bandera suffered a major loss of life and property fourteen years later when the river overran its banks. The townspeople immediately went to work and turned most of the floodplain within the city into open parkland. Today, Bandera is a cultural blend of Indian, Mexican, Polish, and Western cultures, and, although in 1990 the population was only 877 people, the opportunity for tourism, camping, horse racing, and dude ranching makes this town an interesting and historically worthwhile place to visit.

ADVENTURES IN HISTORY

What happens when the major industry in a town dies? More often than not, the town itself dies with it. Not so in the case of this one small feisty town. Left with the dilemma of a declining cattle industry, the town reinvented itself. When you have a bunch of lemons and lemons don't sell, the next best thing is making lemonade. Bandera's "lemonade" turned out to be tourists.

During the last of the great cattle drives, Bandera became known as the cowboy capital of the world. The town consisted of sprawling working ranches where cattle, as well as sheep and goats, made Bandera home. But the local economy declined after 1900 when a series of floods destroyed sawmills, gins, and businesses, and, at the same time, the cattle drives ceased.

In the 1930s, when ranching also fell on hard times and the thin soil made farming a poor alternative, some ranchers decided to take in "dudes," and a brand-new industry was born.

Today Bandera boasts a dozen or more dude ranches that guarantee city slickers a taste of Texas—complete with chuck wagon meals and horse trails alive with armadillos and jackrabbits. Folks from all over the world come to have the "dude" experience. Gone are the cattle drives and farming industry, but Bandera has turned its historic past into the present, maintaining its claim as Cowboy Capital of the World by presenting all the trappings of cowboy times gone by. Bandera's past history is evident as you wander down Main Street. Check out the Old West look of the street peppered with saloons, blacksmiths, old-fashioned soda fountains, and even the 1881 city jail. Summertime is rodeo time with two rodeos a week. Visitors who walk along the former court house lawn find the bronze monument erected to honor the many National Rodeo Champions from Bandera. Bandera's revival style court house is now used as a library. Everywhere you look, Bandera's cowboy history speaks loudly and clearly as cattle drives became rodeos and farms and ranches morphed into dude ranches.

On the Map

Bandera is located on State Highway 16 fifty miles northwest of San Antonio in east central Bandera County.

Weekend Adventures

Bandera offers everything from nature and outdoor activities to nightlife. Stop in at the Cabaret Cafe & Dance Hall on Main Street, going strong since 1936. Take a stroll along the cypress-lined Medina River in Bandera City Park. A visit to St. Stanislaus Catholic Church can also include a walk through the old cemetery, and a moment or two in the meditation garden containing an outdoor Stations of the Cross. Travelers can also spend time horseback riding, fishing, swimming hiking, golfing, and more. Add rodeos, live music, and dance halls, and you have a complete picture of Bandera today.

Bandera, Texas, County Courthouse. Vikk Simmons

Best Time to Visit

If you're planning a trip in July, be sure to work in the annual Texas International Apple Festival held annually along the Medina River. Bandera is also known as the Apple Capital of Texas. Or you can wait until fall to see the stunning fall foliage of the Lost Maples State Natural Area north of Vanderpool and the many species of birds found in the area. Cowboys practice their roping skills at private arenas in the area all during the year.

Adventures in Lodging and Dining

For a real western cowboy happening, try the historic Silver Spur Guest Ranch, one of many dude ranches found in the area. Enjoy western activities at the Flying L Ranch nestled in the heart of the hill country, or head on out to the Mansion in Bandera, a 125-year-old mansion with a carriage house that is now a bed and breakfast. Other guest ranches include the

Running R Ranch, the historic Dixie Dude Ranch, and Mayan Dude Ranch. Restaurants range from the Bandera Ice House to the Cabaret Cafe & Dance Hall, where numerous country stars have performed, such as Willie Nelson and Bob Wills.

FOR MORE INFORMATION

Check with the Bandera County Convention & Visitors Bureau by e-mail at bandera@hctoc.net.

FORT CLARK: THE STORY OF THE U.S. MILITARY IN TEXAS

BRACKETTVILLE, TEXAS

On June 20, 1852, two companies of the First Infantry, accompanied by an advance and rear guard U.S. Mounted Rifles—later renamed the 3rd Cavalry—established Fort Clark at the headwaters of Las Moras Creek in an area now known as Kinney County, Texas, the land of the heroes. Named "The Mulberries" by Spanish explorers, the natural spring had played host to many Indian camps and had been a stopping place along the Comanche War Trail into Mexico.

O. B. Brackett came to Fort Clark and opened the first trading post in a town he called Las Moras. Later called Brackettville, the town earned a real reputation in the late 1800s that rivaled the California Gold Rush towns for gambling, prostitution, and other goings on. During its history, the Fort Clark–Brackettville area nourished many travelers who found the area to be as nurturing an oasis in the Texas southwest as travelers do today.

ADVENTURES IN HISTORY

The story of Fort Clark is the story of the United States military in Texas. Although the Federal soldiers left in 1861, the Second Texas Mounted Rifles remained through August 1862. The fort then became a supply depot and hospital for Confederate troops and local civilians. The most famous inhabitants, the Seminole-Negro Indian Scout Medal of Honor recipients, came to Fort Clark in 1872 and stayed through 1914. Fort Clark is also noted as the headquarters for MacKenzie's raiders. Other occupants have included the famous black "Buffalo Soldiers." After the Indian Wars, Fort Clark remained operational during the Mexican Revolution and through World War I. The fort continued service during World War II with more than twelve thousand troops being trained for the Second Cavalry Division. In fact, the fort also hosted a German prisoner of war subcamp, temporary housing for additional prisoners of war.

Deactivated in 1946, the fort was sold to Brown and Root and later became a guest ranch. In 1971 a private corporation purchased the fort and turned it into a recreational area. Now on twenty-seven hundred acres, Fort Clark has something for everyone. The Las Moras creek banks lure nature lovers with opportunities for bird watching, fishing, picnicking, hiking, and camping. The nine- and eighteen-hole golf courses and two-story stone cavalry barracks turned into modern motel rooms attract many visitors. History buffs will enjoy the National Register Historic District, the military museum, and the fact that much of Fort Clark remains as it was in the 1800s. Visitors enjoy a bit of living history.

On the Map

Located about 120 miles west of San Antonio on U.S. 90, Fort Clark and Brackettville are within easy driving distance of Del Rio, Uvalde, and Eagle Pass.

Weekend Adventures

When visitors approach the fort's entrance, they encounter the Empty Saddle statue. The statue represents both the death of a soldier and the end of the horse cavalry. The Old Guardhouse Museum contains much of the fort's military history. In Brackettville, take in the Kinney Courthouse, built in 1910, and the Kinney County Museum. The Masonic

Lodge building, built in 1879, the original county courthouse, sits next to the Kinney Courthouse. North of Brackettville the Alamo Village, movie set for John Wayne's movie *The Alamo*, lures most people with its cantina-restaurant, trading post, Indian store, authentic stage depot, old time jail, bank, and other buildings. The Seminole-Negro Indian Scout Cemetery where the Medal of Honor recipients are buried is located on Farm Road 3348 west of town.

Best Time to Visit

If you want to experience some military living history, then be sure to schedule a trip during the time of Fort Clark Day held in the fall. The day includes Judge Roy Bean trials, gunfights, and foot races.

Adventures in Lodging and Dining

For an historical overnight stay, try the Las Moras Inn in Brackettville's historical district. You can stay at the fort's 38-room motel, Fort Clark Springs Motel, and the full service RV park. Tent camping is also available. Be sure to call ahead. The Fort Clark Springs Golf Club Snackbar offers a light lunch.

For More Information

If you plan to stay at the fort or are interested in the Fort Clark memberships, contact the Fort Clark Springs Association (www.fortclark.com). Contact the Kinney County Tourism Association, Kinney County Chamber of Commerce, PO Box 386, Brackettville, TX, 78832.

Strawberries and a Comic Strip

Poteet, Texas

Two postmasters had an impact on the small Texan town of Poteet. The first, Francis Marion Poteet, who operated the post office out of his black-

smith shop in 1886, gave the town its name. Henry Mumme, who succeeded Poteet as postmaster in 1896, gave the town its nickname: the
Strawberry City. After a drought ruined Poteet's cotton crop, Mumme discovered artesian wells in the area and began to grow strawberries on his
irrigated land. Strawberries soon became the town's major claim to fame
and in 1948 resulted in a three-day festival that continues to this day.

During the 1950s, the Strawberry City achieved even more acclaim
when Milton Caniff, author of the popular Steve Canyon comic strip,
named one of the characters Poteet. The town remains an agricultural
community with the farming of peanuts, onions, and watermelons as
well as the famous strawberries. Today Poteet is an incorporated city
with more than 3,300 people.

Adventures in History

The time was 1948: World War II had ended, and the soldiers were returning from the front. Proud of its heroes, Poteet wanted to give them
a big welcome. With the town so identified by the strawberry crop, the
Strawberry Festival was a natural outcome.

The Poteet Rotary Club, who also wanted to encourage the veterans
to return to the farms, organized the event. The media, the citizens of
South Texas, and the town became enthusiastic and there were plenty of
festival volunteers. Today, more than eight thousand volunteers come
from all over Texas, neighboring states, and some foreign countries help
to put on the annual Poteet Strawberry Festival. Over the years, the Poteet volunteers became expert berry-packers and made sure the customers would always know how many berries they were receiving by
packing them in a uniform pint, flat, or crate.

With Poteet producing forty percent of Texas's strawberries, the festival continues to be a major economic help for South Texas and Atascosa
County, and a major tourist attraction for the state. The event also pro-
motes Poteet's main agricultural group as well as granting scholarships
for the town's young people. With strawberry auctions, fiddler contests,

dances, and fireworks, the festival promises fun for everyone and lets you know why Poteet is known today as the Strawberry Capital of Texas.

ON THE MAP

Located about twenty miles south of San Antonio on Farm Road 476 and State Highway 16, Poteet is on the Alamo–La Bahia Corridor. This 90-mile corridor parallels the San Antonio River from the Alamo, Mission San Antonio de Valero, to Goliad, Presidio La Bahia, and offers a wonderful journey in historical, cultural, and natural attractions.

WEEKEND ADVENTURES

Although the Poteet Strawberry Festival is the event of the year, make sure you go by the various strawberry monuments that populate the area. One goliath may well be the world's largest strawberry, weighing 1,600 pounds and standing seven feet tall. Not to be outdone, fans of Steve Canyon's comic strip will also find a monument to the comic strip's character, Poteet Canyon. Other strawberry sites include a water tower that sports a painting of a strawberry, stem and all. A megaberry located in front of the Poteet Volunteer Fire Department, proudly declares Poteet the Strawberry Capital of Texas.

BEST TIME TO VISIT

More than 100,000 people attend the Poteet Stawberry Festival every April, usually during the second week. Activities, including Western and Tejano stars, are included in the price of admission, and children under ten are admitted free.

ADVENTURES IN LODGING AND DINING

Although there is no lodging in Poteet, motel accommodations can be found from nine miles away in Pleasanton, Jourdanton to Devine, Lytle, or San Antonio. If you plan to attend the festival, make reservations early. For dining in or take-out, the LBJ Barbeque offers a varied menu including ribs, tacos, and hamburgers. The restaurant is open Tuesday through Sunday.

FOR MORE INFORMATION

Contact the Poteet, Texas, Chamber of Commerce or the folks at the Poteet Strawberry Festival (www.strawberryfestival.com.). For information on the Alamo–La Bahia Corridor, contact the Alamo Area Council of Governments (AACOG) or check the tourism page of their website, www.aacog.com.

SMOKEY JOE, INTO THE HALL OF FAME

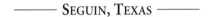

——— SEGUIN, TEXAS ———

The Guadalupe and San Marcos Rivers flow through the city of Seguin, one of the oldest towns in Texas, and the county seat of Guadalupe County. Although the Gonzalez Rangers had named the city Walnut Springs, the name was quickly changed to Seguin to honor the Tejano Juan N. Seguin, known as the Paul Revere of Texas, who served with Sam Houston's Army and was a hero in the fight for Texas independence. Eventually, Seguin worked as a Texas senator and the mayor of San Antonio.

During the years of the Republic of Texas, settlers established cotton plantations, and cotton ruled. Later, the town became a center of several experiments with concrete. Their experimentation paid off when they invented a product called limecrete. Many of the town's structures were made from this material. Only about twenty of these concrete relics survive. One is the Sebastopol State Historic Site. Rich farms and pasture lands, along with cotton, added to the town's prosperity. Already an established city, Seguin became one of the few boomtowns resulting from the discovery of oil. Today the city is a mix of stately old homes and

modern residential developments. And, in an antebellum home surrounded by live oaks and elm trees, the people of Seguin boast that Sam
Houston had slept there.

ADVENTURES IN HISTORY

There are many interesting stories from Seguin. One relates to the work
of Janice Woods Windle who set many episodes of her novel *True
Women* in her hometown of Seguin. But the most fascinating story be-
longs to a little-known black baseball pitcher, Smokey Joe Williams. Before there was Joltin' Joe DiMaggio, there was Smokey Joe. But the
latter's trip to the National Hall of Fame was anything but easy.

Neither Smokey Joe Williams's date of birth, 1885 or 1886, nor the
date of his death, probably 1946, are known for certain. Adding to the
confusion, it seems Smokey lied about his age as he grew older. Some say
his father was black and his mother was a Comanche, but that, too, is not
known for sure. However, there is much that can be verified. According
to material compiled by writer Anne Brawner of the Smokey Joe
Williams Tribute Committee of Seguin and the Heritage Museum,
Smokey began his professional baseball career in San Antonio when he
was twenty years old playing for the Black Broncos. At that time, he received the nickname "Cyclone" for his fastball. He eventually played with
two great Negro League teams, the New York Lincoln Giants and the
Homestead Grays of Pittsburgh. At somewhere between 6 feet 3 inches
and 6 feet 6 inches and around two hundred pounds, he was an athlete's
athlete, pitching in his best year to a recorded forty-one wins and three
losses. He became the most famous black baseball player ever, even beat-
ing out Satchel Paige by one vote for that prestigious title in 1952.

Although segregation reigned in those days, and Joe Williams was
never allowed to play for one of the white major league teams, he
pitched in some exhibition games against white teams. He compiled a
lifetime record of 19-7 or 20-7, depending on the source. And two of
those losses came when he was forty-five years old. In 1917, he struck

out twenty batters in a no-hitter against the New York Giants. After that game, Ross Youngs, a future Hall of Famer, said, "Nice game, Smokey," and the name stuck. Williams retired in 1932 and tended bar in Harlem until he died. In recent years Smokey Joe's achievements have been compared to those of Nolan Ryan, another famous Texas baseball player. In July 1999, Smokey Joe Williams was finally inducted into the Baseball Hall of Fame.

ON THE MAP

Seguin is located in South Central Texas on Interstate 10 and is 30 miles east of San Antonio. The ports of Houston and Corpus Christi are nearly equal distance from Seguin.

WEEKEND ADVENTURES

There are numerous historical sites in Seguin, and many nineteenth- and twentieth-century homes. The art deco courthouse is found in the downtown historic district, and the Juan Seguin statue is located in the heart of downtown. His burial and a stone recounting his life are found on a hillside across from the coliseum. Look for the historical marker. Travelers can wander through the many pre–Texas Revolution buildings, all designated by historical markers.

Check out the Los Nogales Museum containing Texas historical papers, pictures, and furniture. Another sight to see is the Sebastopol House State Historic Site. Built in the early 1850s by slaves of Col. Joshua Young, and recently restored, the site has exhibits that recount the history of the house. The Seguin Conservation Society and the Chamber of Commerce offer the "True Women" tour. This trip down memory lane reflects the lives of the pioneer women in Seguin depicted by author Janice Woods Windle. For a view of the town's historic natural beauty, a visit to the Walnut Springs Memorial Rose Garden is in order.

BEST TIME TO VISIT

For those interested in fine homes of the past, travel to Seguin on the first weekend of December when the Heritage Tour of Homes, sponsored by the Seguin Conservation Society displays some of the nineteenth-century and early twentieth-century old homes. On the second weekend in October, enjoy the Guadalupe County Fair and Rodeo, and in November there's the Pecan Fest.

ADVENTURES IN LODGING AND DINING

The historic Weinert House Bed and Breakfast is a Queen Anne Victorian home built in 1895. Another place to stay is the Bartoskewitz Farmhouse Bed and Breakfast that offers insight into the heritage of ranching and farming in Texas. It presents an opportunity to feed lambs and look at old and new farming equipment as you watch agriculture in operation today. Or choose lodging at the Texas Agriculture and Heritage Center with its hundred-year-old home used for the bed and breakfast. Stop by to see how the old west and the agriculture industry progressed until today. In the historic district downtown, try Guadalupe Grille on S. Austin. For barbecue, head out to Davila's BBQ on Highway 123.

FOR MORE INFORMATION

For information and/or self-guided tour information on the historical sites in Seguin, visit the Seguin Area Chamber of Commerce website at http://seguintx.org.

CREATING THE INDIANOLA TRAIL

——— YORKTOWN ———

If you're a Texas history buff traveling down the old Indianola Trail, be sure to stop in Yorktown, DeWitt County's oldest incorporated town.

This town grew slowly from its beginning in 1848 when Captain John York, the famous Indian fighter, and his good friend Charles Eckhardt decided to build a place where their families could settle. When the Aransas Pass Railway was built a mile to the south, folks picked up and relocated near the railroad, and for a while they called it Upper Yorktown. In the ensuing years, Yorktown thrived with its share of gristmills, dance halls, and hotels. By 1898, Yorktown had more than sixty owners in various businesses, and in 1918 the Chamber of Commerce formed.

By the hundredth anniversary, Yorktown had a city park, library, and fire station, and by 1990, the city's population had grown to more than two thousand. Today Yorktown is known for the great opportunity to pick up your binoculars and find various varieties of butterflies and birds. Or take advantage of exceptional wild game hunting.

ADVENTURES IN HISTORY

Meet Charles Eckhardt and Captain John York, the visionaries who founded and expanded the Indianola Trail. In keeping with the ethnic diversity of the time, Eckhardt arrived from Laasphe, Germany, in 1832 and settled in the major Texas seaport of Indianola. Although business was booming, getting and shipping goods meant travel over rough trails. Eckhardt had an idea. What if he obtained a survey for a road from Indianola through Yorktown to New Braunfels? He put his plan into action, and from the time it opened, the new trail became an important part of business and established Yorktown as a significant relay station for all sorts of transportation users from trail drivers to mail and passengers. Eckhardt had created the Old Indianola Trail.

The story goes that Eckhardt met John York, probably during their military service in the Texas War of Independence, and they became good friends. For his service, Captain York received acres of land in the Coleto Creek area. In 1846, while Eckhardt was still in Indianola, York moved to Coleto Creek. Two years later, he and Eckhardt established Yorktown a short distance away. Wanting to enhance the value of his land, York established a settlement. History tells us that in 1848, the founders offered land to the first ten families to settle the region. Many German, Bohemian, and Polish families arrived and took advantage of the offer, thereby changing the wilderness into a prosperous community. Although York moved to the area first, it was Eckhardt who had the first house built in Yorktown in 1848. However, he never lived to see the town he built develop into the bustling place it was to become. He died of yellow fever at sea. Although he had no children, his brother, Caesar Eckhardt, occupied the house and created a mercantile company known as the leading firm of its kind in western DeWitt County.

Captain York also did not have the joy of seeing the land he fought so hard for develop beyond its very beginnings. In October of 1848, Captain York and his son-in-law, James Madison Bell, were killed in a battle with marauding Indians and were buried together in the same handmade coffin. York, however, had ten children who saw the town grow and prosper. Eckhardt moved away after York's death. The town received the name of York in honor of Captain York.

On the Map

Located on State Highway 72 and Coleto Creek, Yorktown is in the southwest portion of DeWitt County, and is about 75 miles east of San Antonio and 36 miles northwest of Victoria.

Weekend Adventures

First a tent, then built of logs, Charles Eckhardt's first store finally evolved to a building of sandstone and steel. Fully restored in 1985, the building now houses the Yorktown Historical Museum and is listed on the National Register of Historic Places. According to Melissa Armstrong, Executive Director of the Yorktown Chamber of Commerce, "This museum offers Texas' only known indoor water cistern. This cistern supplied a water source for settlers seeking protection from Indian attacks, such as the one with the Lipan Apache Indians in which Captain York was killed."

The Historical Homes tours are self-guided and show many structures dating back to the mid-to-late 1800s. While in town, drive by the Lutheran Church and take a gander at the enormous oak tree, one of the oldest in the state.

BEST TIME TO VISIT

Head out to Yorktown the third weekend in October in time for the annual Yorktown Western Days, or take in the town's annual Fiesta En La Calle the first Saturday in April. Other events include the Yorktown Independence Day Celebration in July and the First Saturday Traders Market (April through December).

ADVENTURES IN LODGING AND DINING

The Pecan Tree Inn Bed & Breakfast, built in 1920, is located for convenience only one block north of main street and shopping. At this inn, you can rock on the chairs on its wrap-around porch or take pleasure in the peace and quiet of a walk through the pecan trees. Enjoy C&A 3 Oaks Guest Ranch as you hike in the pastures or stroll down by the creek and watch the different species of birds and animals go by. Restaurants include Schultz's Family Dining Restaurant and the Coleto Creek Emporium Restaurant & Gift Shop, a nice place to go for a cup of coffee in the morning, meet with friends for lunch break, or even sip high tea served in the late afternoon.

FOR MORE INFORMATION

Contact the Yorktown Chamber of Commerce & Agriculture (www.yorktowntx.com).

6

In and Around the Texas Gulf Coast

The Texas Gulf Coast area is known as a recreational playground for Texans and the nation, an over-fly area for migratory birds, and a land dedicated to conservation and preservation. Galveston, once the largest city in Texas, continues to lure people to her streets to enjoy the beaches; Corpus Christi is one of the most popular vacation spots in Texas. But life on the Gulf Coast has not always been so pleasant.

Before the settlers inhabited the land, bands of Atakapas and the Karankawas roamed the marshes, hunting and living a nomadic life. The number of towns that have come and gone is legendary and include Velasco and Indianola. The devastation of flood waters and the pounding of hurricanes have left their mark not only on the land but on the people, and in doing so, on the history. The impact of the 1900 storm on Galveston Island still makes news today. Over six thousand people were killed in what is still considered to be the United States's worst natural disaster.

For generations, Padre Island and other coastal points brought sailing ships to their ruin. Chief among the examples is the story of French explorer La Salle and the wreck of *La Belle*, one of La Salle's ships. La

Salle's journey is a sorry one and ends with the explorer being murdered by his own men. Shipwrecks and tales of pirate treasure weave through this era of maritime exploration, and the Texas coast has long been the source of legends and lore. The pirate Lafitte made Galveston his home port for a number of years. Even today treasure hunters search for the elusive Spanish galleons, loaded with treasure, that fell into the pirate's hands.

Although some wrecks that lie deep in the offshore waters succumbed to the violent storms of the coastal area, others were the result of war. Today the waterlogged remains of the Union gunboat, USS *Hatteras,* lie off the coast of Galveston, and the site is listed in the National Register of Historic Places. During World War II, groups of German U-boats, known as wolf packs, patrolled the Gulf shores. Even today rumors of a German submarine that went down off the Texas coast persist. For many long-time residents, San Luis Pass is known as the graveyard of wrecked ships.

The Gulf coast area is a haven for Texas maritime museums. The battleship *Texas,* now part of the San Jacinto Battleground State Park, brings contemporary maritime history alive. The La Salle Shipwreck Project, a collection of seven sister museums, highlights La Salle's fateful journey, and includes the museums of Port Isabelle, the National Museum of the Pacific War in Fredericksburg, Sea Wolf Park on Pelican Island, the Texas Maritime Museum in Rockport, the Texas Seaport Museum, the tall ship *Elissa* in Galveston, and the USS *Lexington* Museum on the Bay in Corpus Christi. Not only is the USS *Lexington* docked in the city, but replicas of the ships of Columbus can also be found moored at the C. Storm Pavilion under the Harbor Bridge. South Padre Island offers history-hunters the Port Isabel Lighthouse State Historical Park.

Today the coastal towns of Padre Island, Corpus Christi, and Galveston beckon travelers to their shores for days and weeks loaded with summer fun and southern hospitality, but for history buffs, beach lovers, and shell-seekers, the Texas Gulf Coast is a true treasure-trove.

WHY U. S. GRANT GREW A BEARD

CORPUS CHRISTI

Corpus Christi began life in 1519 when, on the Roman Catholic Feast Day of Corpus Christi, the Spanish explorer Alonzo Alvarez de Pineda discovered a bay on the southern coast of Texas. Named for the feast day, the city of Corpus Christi started out as a frontier trading post and remained an obscure settlement until July 1845 when U.S. troops under General Zachary Taylor arrived and set up camp to prepare for the war with Mexico. Because the camp was now a city, it took the name Corpus Christi first bestowed upon it those many years ago when it was just a piece of land on a semi-tropical bay. The city's first ordinance in 1879 made illegal letting hogs and goats run loose.

Today, the place Pineda discovered so long ago is the largest city on the Texas coast, and the sixth largest port in the nation. Each spring it is also home to the nation's largest marathon race of one thousand teams comprised of six runners each. In 2003, the National Civic League selected Corpus Christi, one of ten cities nationwide and the only one in Texas, as an All-American City. But many years ago, a soldier named Grant, discovered a town he fell in love with, the same Corpus Christi.

ADVENTURES IN HISTORY

In 1845, future general Ulysses S. Grant was a handsome young lieutenant with a smooth, clean-shaven face. In fact, his fellow officers often called him "Beauty." Grant accompanied Zachary Taylor when he was ordered to Corpus Christi in July of that year. Grant loved this small town, especially the abundance of cheap horses, and soon acquired three mustangs. However that pleasure was short-lived when his free black servant took them to water and they got away. In September of that year this future general, but for a quirk of fate, almost had no future at all. Grant had planned to take a trip on the *Dayton*, but changed his mind at the last moment. In a letter he wrote his fiancée, he told her the boilers on the *Dayton* had exploded killing nine men.

Later that winter, Lt. Grant and the other young men built a theater and planned the production of Shakespeare's *Othello*. Although they had no problem casting men, no one would play Desdemona. But Grant, whom the officers continued to call "Beauty," fit into the Desdemona costume perfectly, and the men persuaded him to try out for the role. Eventually, they gave up on Grant when the officer who played the Moor couldn't look at Grant without laughing. Finally, they sent to New Orleans for a professional actress to relieve Grant and play Desdemona.

After that fiasco, Grant grew a beard.

On the Map

Corpus Christi is located on the Gulf Coast at the junction of Interstate 37 and U.S. Highways 77 and 181, 210 miles southwest of Houston.

Weekend Adventures

There is a lot to see in the city and the surrounding area. Corpus Christi is home to the USS *Lexington* and the Museum on the Bay, as well as the Columbus Fleet. Docked next to the Corpus Christi Museum of Science and History, the Columbus Fleet consists of replicas of the *Niña*, *Pinta*, and *Santa Maria*, all reproductions of the famous sailing vessels, as well as other special exhibits. The USS *Lexington*, also called the "Blue Ghost," is a 910-foot aircraft carrier that served the country from 1943 during World War II to 1991. Now the ship is a museum and home to many restored airplanes, educational and historical exhibits, and collections.

Historical landmarks also include the 1914 Nueces County Courthouse, Old St. Anthony's Catholic Church, and archeological sites such as the Tucker and the Oso Dune sites containing Karankawa Indian artifacts. The Heritage Park and Multicultural Center has nine Victorian homes and offers cultural programs all year round. The city's oldest home, the Centennial House, built in 1848, was once a Civil War hospital. Captain Clark's flagship, a four hundred–passenger paddle wheeler, will take you on tours of the bay and port. The Selena Museum, a tribute to the famous Hispanic singer slain at early age, is one of the newest of Corpus Christi's historical and cultural sites.

BEST TIME TO VISIT

Corpus Christi has approximately 255 days of sunshine each year. Any time is a good time, and activities are plentiful in this Gulf Coast town. Visitors can enjoy the annual Harbor Lights Festival in the beginning of December when dozens of boats sail forth and lights twinkle in reflection on the water with the lighting of a 75-foot tree at sunset.

ADVENTURES IN LODGING AND DINING

There are a number of historic bed and breakfasts in Corpus Christi. The George Blucher House Bed and Breakfast Inn is designated an historic galleried Victorian home, one that displays elegance and extends a hearty Southern welcome to visitors. The owners of Ocean House bed and breakfast call their B&B a memory in the making with its refurbished 1936 contemporary Mediterranean-styled main house surrounded by a tropical garden and a view of Corpus Christi bay from private balconies.

Just over the JFK Bridge visit a variety of seafood restaurants where you can sit, dine, and watch the sun set over the Lagoona Madre. Snoopy's, Frenchy's, and the JFK Bridge Restaurant's menus offer local fish.

FOR MORE INFORMATION

Contact the Corpus Christi Convention & Visitors Bureau at their website (www.corpuschristichamber.org/). For historical information, check out the Corpus Christi Landmark Commission (www.cclandmarks.org).

FLOWERS AND FEUDS

CUERO

When their homes and businesses were destroyed by the devastating weather in Indianola, oxcarts hauled what little goods the people had left to Cuero. At that time in Cuero's history, cattle were the mainstay of the area, and the settlers herded them across the Arroyo del Cuero, meaning rawhide in Spanish. Cuero had become a major route for many cattle drives, and this is the place where the famed Chisholm Trail began. Lawlessness, including cattle rustling, was rampant during the late 1800s. Women and children could not go out after dark. Turkeys, an important product of the area, made the town one of the largest poultry markets in the Southwest. In 1912 Cuero put on the first Turkey Trot parade.

Today De Witt County numbers among the counties in Texas with the most cattle. Turkeys have gone the way of the dodo bird. Except for the annual Turkeyfest, when the folks in Cuero do talk turkey and award the Traveling Turkey Trophy of Tumultuous Triumph—all four feet of it—to the winner of the Great Gobbler Gallop. Cuero is a classic Texas town, one that is proud of its history and its legacy, a town that's looking to the future.

ADVENTURES IN HISTORY

Although Cuero bills itself as the Wildflower Capital of Texas because of the more than one hundred different species, it is also home to the longest running and bloodiest feud in Texas history. After the Civil War, lawlessness reigned, and the Sutton-Taylor feud grew from those bad days. No one really knows the exact cause. Although the feud lasted for thirty years, the discussion has lasted for more than a hundred years.

One tale claims the families came from another state and continued the strife in Texas, but there's never been any proof to support this theory. The Hatfields and McCoys had nothing on this feuding family group. The Taylors were fond of shooting anyone they disagreed with, or merely anyone they didn't like. In 1868 they ran afoul of the law when William Sutton, a deputy sheriff, led a posse in pursuit of horse thieves and one of his men caught and killed a Taylor.

According to the first family of Taylors, from whom the feud took its name, it really started when Buck Taylor accused a Sutton of dishonesty in the sale of some horses. The Taylors became involved because of the Sutton's connection to the state police. The killing spiraled downhill from there, resulting in the state police terrorizing a large part of Southeast Texas. People were accused of trivial charges and assassinated. When one of the Taylors heard a ringing cowbell in his cornfield and went out to investigate, he was shot to death.

The family responded by avenging his death, and so the feud continued with lynchings and shootings. Most notable was a Taylor's escape from jail in Indianola as a result of the great storm of 1875. The country fell into confusion, and people were forced to take sides. Death was violent and frequent. And so the killing went on. Even when the men who perpetrated the last of the feud killings were brought to justice, legal maneuvers lasted over twenty years and resulted in a single conviction, and that person was pardoned.

ON THE MAP

Cuero is located where U.S. Highways 183, 77A, and 87 bump into each other in central DeWitt County.

WEEKEND ADVENTURES

Cuero is rich in history and has fifty structures on the National Register of Historic Places, and more than sixty of its homes display a historical marker. Main Street is made up of three historic districts. The 1896 courthouse, complete with a belfry, is listed as a Texas Historical Landmark and is on the National Registry of Historic Structures. The Cuero Heritage

Museum has everything you want to know about the history of the town's turkeys and Turkeyfest. Explore a part of history in the DeWitt County Historical Museum on Broadway. The museum, in the Bates-Sheppard Home, was shipped in pieces after the 1886 hurricane devastated Indianola and was reconstructed in Cuero. The Reuss Pharmacy Museum brings history alive with everything from glass bottles, many of them still containing ingredients, to the museum's centerpiece, an antique soda fountain. The Historic Federal Building of Cuero houses the Cuero Heritage Museum and the Chamber of Commerce and Agriculture.

Best Time to Visit

Don't miss the Cuero Turkeyfest, held on the second full weekend in October each year. This event takes place as the North Star or Worthington, Minnesota, and the Lone Star, Cuero, Texas, come together for a friendly rivalry of the Great Gobbler Gallop. Folks watch to see which Turkey claims the title and bragging rights for their city as the Turkey Capital of the World. Photographers, wildflower enthusiasts, and artists will want to check out Cuero's country lanes during Wildflower Month in April.

Adventures in Lodging and Dining

The Broadway House Bed & Breakfast is a restored home believed to have been either built or moved to its present site in 1889. Wildflower Inn is a renovated two-story bed and breakfast decorated in antique style and built around 1916. The owners invite you to stay and experience life the way it was in a simpler time. For those who enjoy gourmet dining, the Secret Garden Tea Room on Esplanade Street may have just the meal.

For More Information

Contact the Chamber of Commerce at their website at www.cuero.org. For more information on the Turkeyfest, go online to www.turkeyfest

.org. To learn more about the De Witt County wildflowers, contact www.dewittwildflowers.org.

FINDING THE LOST CITY OF VELASCO

——— FREEPORT ———

Freeport is a city that owes its life, in large part, to a company. Although the town had a post office in 1898, it didn't come into its own until 1912 when the world's largest sulfur mines, Freeport Sulfur Company, dedicated the town. From a one-room schoolhouse in 1914, Freeport has grown considerably due to the construction of the Dow Chemical Company facilities in 1939 and to the town's becoming part of the Brazosport industrial area. In 1957, Velasco became a part of Freeport when it was incorporated into the town.

Quintana, Texas's oldest seaport, saw its first colonists when Stephen F. Austin landed in 1822. Plantation families enjoyed Quintana as a favorite vacation spot, and fine homes dotted the ridge of the beach. Storms tore at Quintana repeatedly, as they did the sister city of Velasco. Once a major port, the town suffered a major blow with the building of the Gulf Intracoastal Waterway. Today, with its tiny population, Quintana is still a popular place for beachgoers and the site of Brazoria County Park.

ADVENTURES IN HISTORY

Although the Seven Museums of the La Salle Odyssey claim *La Belle*, and Port Lavaca has a connection to the Confederate submarine, *Hunley*, the first to sink a warship, Freeport has its own maritime story. In his book, *Texas' Liberty Ships: From World War II Working-Class Heroes to Artificial Reefs*, marine archeologist Barto Arnold of Texas A&M University discusses the importance of mass produced ships used in World War II to carry cargo and troops. The United States was engaged in a race and building ships as quickly as possible to replace damage done by the German

U-boats. When the war ended, some of these Liberty Ships were put in reserve; however, others continued, helping in the Korean War. By the 1970s they were too old to use. Although a few were scrapped, many were, like old horses, put out to pasture, or in this instance, put out to oceans.

Because the bottom of the ocean on the Texas coast is essentially sand and mud, there's nothing solid, so coral and other plants and animals are unable to build reefs. By sinking ships in Texas waters at places like Freeport, the Texas Parks and Wildlife supply a habitat for coral and barnacles to grow and become the base of a food chain. Once more in service, the Liberty Ships now are an environmental addition to Texas's historical heritage.

Although in 1957, Velasco became a part of Freeport, it has since been determined that the site of Fort Velasco was in Surfside Beach near City Hall, but a portion also is located on the other side of the Freeport Channel within the Town of Quintana. Today Old Velasco's history has melded into the history of Freeport, Quintana, and Surfside Beach, now resort-recreation areas.

On the Map

Located on the upper Texas coast in Brazoria County, Freeport is about 50 miles south of Houston where the Brazos River meets the Texas Gulf Coast. Galveston is about thirty miles north. Surfside Beach can be found in Brazoria County five miles from Freeport. Quintana is on the other side of the Freeport Channel from Surfside Beach, located on the west side of the mouth of the Brazos River and on Farm Roads 1495 and 723.

Weekend Adventures

For a bit of fun and history, check out *Mystery*, a former shrimp boat trawler, on display at the head of Brazosport Harbor channel on Texas 288. The monument honors the historic shrimp industry of the Brazosport area. Extensive facilities for both inshore and deep-sea fishing are also available. Quintana Beach County Park has two historic homes. Coveney House features a period museum and natural history display, and Seabum House is home for the park office. The park's recreational facilities on the island include paved, elevated boardwalks, off-beach parking, shaded pavilions, rest rooms, showers, a multilevel fishing pier, and a playground. For more history, head to nearby Lake Jackson and relive the past at the Lake Jackson Historical Museum.

Many conservationists, nature lovers, and birders enjoy the area at Surfside, and Quintana beaches are nationally known roosting grounds for migratory birds. The highest national 12-hour bird count ever taken was in Brazosport area in 1973 with 226 species.

BEST TIME TO VISIT

Certainly the summer would be the best time to visit the beaches, and with more than six hundred shell species, shell-seekers are sure to be happy. In December, birders will enjoy the Freeport Audubon Christmas Bird Count, one of the top ranked bird counts nationally for the numbers of species. Birders return annually in hopes of seeing a new record set.

ADVENTURES IN LODGING AND DINING

There are plenty of places to stay in all three locations. In Freeport try the Freeport Inn or Gulf Crest Motel. In Surfside Beach there's the Surfside Motel and Cedar Sands Motel, or visitors might want to rent a beach house in Quintana. Try the Quintana Rose located only a couple of blocks from the beach and enjoy a great view of the gulf. The Quintana Light House is situated across the street from the Neotropical Bird Sanctuary and about six blocks from the shipping canal.

Food is abundant in all the areas. In Quintana, the Jetty's casual dining offers a great view of the gulf and shipping canal. In Surfside, remember a picnic at the beach is always memorable.

FOR MORE INFORMATION

To discover more about these sites, contact the Brazosport Area Chamber of Commerce at their website www.brazosport.org or email chamber@brazosport.org. For more information on Quintana, find the website www.quintana-tx.org/aboutquintana.htm.

THE BIRTHPLACE OF JUNETEENTH

──── GALVESTON ISLAND ────

Rich in history and in story, Galveston Island is full of tales of tragedy and high drama. The fact that anywhere from six to eight thousand souls were lost during the raging 1900 storm is enough to fuel imaginations for a long time. Known to have been home to the infamous pirate Jean Lafitte, the island has worn the labels of Wall Street of the Southwest, Little Ellis Island, and the "Richest City in Texas." During the 1890s Galveston was high society and on the verge of becoming one of the nation's major ports. In fact, the island city had been in a race with Houston for the honor, and Galveston was moving ahead. Then the big storm hit the island and blanketed the land in water. When the water receded, the beaches, with pyres of dead bodies, became crematoriums.

Galveston did not recover until the next century. In the '20s, '30s, and '40s the city reclaimed her top resort status, and gambling reigned with famous nightclubs such as the Balinese Room and the Hollywood Dinner Club. Throughout its long history, Galveston has remained loyal to the annual Juneteeth Celebration, and the results have been the emergence of a national event that stretches from California to Washington, D.C.

ADVENTURES IN HISTORY

The story begins on June 19, 1865, in Galveston, Texas, when Union General Gordon Granger delivered the Third Order of the Emancipation Proclamation announcing that the war had ended and the slaves were freed: "The people of Texas are informed that in accordance with a Proclamation from the Executive of the United States, all slaves are free."

The streets were filled with the dancing of now-former slaves. The date of June 19th evolved into Juneteenth, and the city of Galveston has celebrated Juneteenth every year since the general's reading.

For a long time, many have questioned why it took so long for Texas to get the news. President Lincoln actually signed the proclamation on January 1, 1863, two and a half years earlier. Some say enforcement was delayed due to the cotton harvest; others blame it on a messenger having been murdered on his way to deliver the news; and still others lay the blame at the feet of the plantation owners. No news meant they could maintain their labor force. No one knows for sure. Today the answer seems to lie in the fact that Texas was so isolated from the rest of the nation at the time.

Once freed, some of the slaves moved north, others moved to Houston, to an area known as Freedtown, and some remained on the plantations and continued to work but were employees instead of slaves. One thing the people did not do: they did not forget.

Every year since 1865, Juneteenth has been celebrated in Galveston. Gradually the celebration moved into Houston and across Texas, and stretched across the nation, ultimately reaching thirty-seven states and counting.

Today Galveston's Juneteenth is one of the city's major celebrations along with the annual Mardi Gras and Dickens on the Strand weekend in early December. The Juneteenth Emancipation Trail Ride, an annual pilgrimage that has grown in number of participants and in miles, begins at Houston's Acres Homes Equestrian Center and ends in Galveston where the trail riders become a part of the annual parade. Each year one mile is added to the journey to mark the new year. The day's events include the reading of the Proclamation of Emancipation at Ashton Villa, the annual March and Prayer Service, the Annual Gospel Celebration, and the Jubilee Parade.

On the Map

Galveston is about fifty miles south of Houston, located on a barrier island two miles off the upper Texas coast. Travelers take Interstate 45 south that leads directly to the island.

Weekend Adventures

A trip to the island is incomplete without a stroll along the historical district known as the Strand or a visit to the Bishop's Palace. Numbering in the top one hundred homes in the nation for its architectural significance, the palace is a place to behold. Galveston has more than 555 designated historical landmarks and more than 1,500 historic homes. The Rosenberg Library provides a somber reminder of Galveston's infamous date, September 8, 1900, with its storm exhibit detailing the nation's deadliest disaster, the Great Storm.

For added fun, take in the Galveston Island outdoor musicals. The Grand 1894 Opera House is known as the Official Opera House of Texas and listed on the National Register of Historic Places. For family fun, a stop at Moody Gardens should be on the list of things to do.

Best Time to Visit

Visitors tend to flock to Galveston in the summer to enjoy the beaches; however, there is more than enough to do in the city to warrant a visit any time during the year. Coordinate a visit in December with the annual Dickens on the Strand weekend or during the first of the year to take advantage of Mardi Gras time. Historical homes, museums, and island tours are available year-round, and any time is a good time for a good old-fashioned trolley or carriage ride 'round the island. For a different view of the island, take the Old Colonial Paddlewheeler, charter a boat, take a cruise, plan a Duck Tour, or try a harbor tour. If birding is your game, the island is ranked among the top birding locations in the nation and their annual Featherfest should top your list.

ADVENTURES IN LODGING AND DINING

Treemont House, located in the historical district known as the Strand, and the Hotel Galvez offer top notch accommodations. As a resort, a wide range of accommodations stretch down the island from motels to condos, and bed and breakfasts to hotels.

Voted the Best Continental in Galveston by Galveston.com's visitors, the Steakhouse is part of the San Luis Resort. Fisherman's Wharf is hailed by *Texas Monthly* as the premier restaurant of the Texas Gulf Coast. For many, a trip to Galveston often includes a visit to Gaido's Seafood Restaurant where dining has been a generational experience.

FOR MORE INFORMATION

The city of Galveston maintains a helpful website at www.galveston.com with maps, directions to the city from both Hobby and Bush International airports, historical information, and much more. The Galveston Historical Foundation (www.galvestonhistory.org) is Texas's oldest historic preservation group. Try www.galvestonislandTX.com for another resource.

AN ANGEL ATTENDS A MASSACRE

——— GOLIAD ———

Every Texan is familiar with the battle cry, "Remember the Alamo," but at the Battle of San Jacinto, the men also rallied to another cry, "Remember Goliad." One of the oldest Spanish colonial municipalities in Texas, Goliad is the county seat of Goliad County. Although the Spanish were first to inhabit the area, the town was later established as La Bahía when its colonizer, José de Escandón, came up with the idea to

move two missions from the Guadalupe River to a site on the San Antonio River. On a hill where the settlers could gather sand, limestone,
and timber, they built this new presidio. On the opposite bank folks
could see Mission Espíritu Santo. In 1829, the town became Goliad, an
anagram of Father Hidalgo, the priest who started the movement for
Mexican independence.

As the railroad steamed into the area in the late 1800s, the town grew,
a new courthouse was built, and local farmers raised cotton and cattle.
But as with many of the Texas towns at that time, trouble dogged the
farmers with the advent of the Great Depression. After the Depression
was over, the city rebounded slowly. The population increased over time,
and the city now has many tourists enjoying the charm of its surroundings and the delights of its history. In 1976, Goliad's downtown square
was listed in the National Register of Historic Places. Goliad's past may
be bloody, but the calm breeze, quiet beauty, and historic treasures of
this picturesque town are its true legacy.

Mission Espíritu Santo Goliad. Elaine L. Galit

ADVENTURES IN HISTORY

Shakespeare once wrote, "What's in a name? That which we call a rose by any other name would smell as sweet." The Angel of Goliad appears to have many names depending on whose history you believe. However, no matter the actual name of this Mexican heroine, her help and compassion at the Battle of Goliad are legendary. About 370 men met their deaths, including Colonel James Fannin, even though Fannin had surrendered to Santa Anna. Mexican Centralist forces ordered the prisoners of Goliad spared, but Santa Anna overrode the order. On Palm Sunday in 1836, 342 men, including Fannin, were massacred.

Dr. Jack Shackelford, a survivor of the Goliad Massacre, refers to the Angel as Pacheta Alevesco. Others have called her Francita, Francisca, Panchita, or Pancheta/Panchita with a last name of Alavez, Alvarez, or Alevesco. Many were saved due to her efforts. Not only had she persuaded

Courthouse tower, Goliad. Elaine L. Galit

Colonel Garay to spare twenty doctors, interpreters, nurses and mechanics, but she also slipped into the fortress during the night and smuggled the Texans out by ones and twos and hid them. She borrowed the young drummer boy to help her for a few minutes, then lost him thus saving his life. She even dragged a wounded man left for dead onto the San Antonio riverbank and dressed his wounds. Santa Anna's terrible butchery fueled Americans' anger throughout the country. Before long, money and more volunteers streamed into Texas. Santa Anna's actions had set the wheels in motion for his own downfall.

Pacheta is often referred to as the wife of Captain Telesforo Alavéz, commander of the forces under General Urrea's command until May 14. On that date, the army withdrew to Matamoros after their defeat at San Jacinto. It was originally believed that Pacheta returned with her husband to Mexico and was abandoned by him. She then came back to Matamoras where the Texians, who knew of her compassionate exploits, took her in. From there she disappeared into the history books. Generations later a relative surfaced at the King Ranch. A teacher on the King Ranch translated the story of the butchery at Goliad for her ranch hand students. One of them, Matias, told her his story. Pacheta, whom he called Francisca, was his mother whom he brought with him when he went to work on the King Ranch. According to family recollections, she passed away at the ranch and was buried there in an unmarked grave. It's believed that Captain King and Mrs. King knew who she was, but respected her desire to remain anonymous.

Although she died in her nineties, Pacheta left an incredible legacy in Texas. Matias had fathered eight children. Numbering among her descendants are a former president of Texas Tech University and the first Hispanic to serve in the United States cabinet under President George H. W. Bush. Francisca Panchita Alavez, also called Pacheta, is the only person on the Mexican side of the Texas fight for independence to be honored by Texas. A life-size bronze statue of Pacheta was sculpted by Houston-area artist Che Rickman and now stands in the Angel of Goliad Plaza, soon to be part of a new hike and bike trail in Goliad State Historical Park. The compassion of the angel of mercy shines through as she poses with one hand over her heart and the other upraised and outstretched to help.

On the Map

Goliad is the gateway to Mexico or the beaches of the Gulf Coast. It is located at the crossroads of Highways 59 and 77A/183. Presidio La Bahia, Goliad's fort, is one mile south of Goliad on Highway 183.

Weekend Adventures

With over 250 years of history behind the town, Goliad has many worthy sites to see. Settled on the San Antonio River, Goliad State Historical Park is the point where history and culture blend and serves as a hub for visiting the many historic sites in and around Goliad.

Start out at Presidio La Bahia, the fort, a National Historic Landmark and the most fought over fort in Texas, where Goliad history began. The echoes of Six National Revolutions and wars for independence are contained within its walls. East of Goliad is a 13.6-acre park, the Fannin Battleground State Historic Site. On this site, Colonel J. W. Fannin surrendered to General Jose Urrea with 284 of his men after the Battle of Coleto. Just east of the Presidio La Bahia visitors find the Fannin Memorial Monument marking the burial site of Fannin and his men. A statue honoring General Ignacio Zaragoza, who defeated the French in 1862, reminds visitors of the reason for the annual Cinco de Mayo celebration.

Start the Downtown Goliad tour with the Market House Museum and Visitor Center. Perhaps Doris Freer, a warm, friendly, and knowledgeable member of the Goliad County Historical Commission, will point out the Hanging Tree (or trees as the case may be) that fan out across the river and around the 1894 courthouse. Most associate one tree with the hanging tree, but Freer says, "the vigilantes just hung them on the best tree wherever they were." She also smiles when she mentions how the old city jail has now become the tax office. Be sure to visit the Mission Espíritu Santo with the remnants of an original wall, priest's quarters, and ruins of the living quarters.

Goliad World War II marker honors the war's veterans. Elaine L. Galit

The Goliad Hanging Trees. Elaine L. Galit

BEST TIME TO VISIT

Goliad has a number of celebrations, including Market Days, Cinco de Mayo Celebration, and the Living History Weekend. For an energetic way to explore history, participate in Goliad's Annual Tour de Goliad Bike Ride on the third Saturday of October. The route takes you by each of the historic locations within the Goliad community. Another great event is during the fourth weekend in March when Goliad holds its Annual Reenactment at the Presidio. Goliad has a great Cinco de Mayo Celebration, too, with a fiesta featuring Mexican food and music.

ADVENTURES IN LODGING AND DINING

For lodging with a historic slant, head to The Quarters at Presidio La Bahia where you can rent a room within the Presidio. According to Chief Ranger Wilfred Korth, a visitor could "have the grounds to yourself at

Goliad Courthouse. Elaine L. Galit

night, and possibly see the ghost they say wanders the grounds." Or try the Antlers Inn, a traditional small-town hotel.

The Blue Quail Deli, the 2003 Taste of Victoria winner of the Best Flavor award recently featured in *Texas Highways Magazine*, combines great food and a casual atmosphere. Try the award-winning cream of jalapeño soup. For a change of pace, and a variety of menu items, head out to the Empresario. Both restaurants are located on the historic town square.

FOR MORE INFORMATION

Contact the Goliad Chamber of Commerce (www.goliadcc.org). To learn more about the Angel of Goliad, go to www.tamu.edu/ccbn/dewitt/goliad angel.htm.

Street in Courthouse Square, Goliad. Elaine L. Galit

FROM COUNTY SEAT TO FISHERMAN'S PARADISE

MATAGORDA

Stephen F. Austin used all his persuasive powers to convince Mexico a military post was needed to protect the incoming settlers. Thus the town of Matagorda was born, the third oldest Anglo town in Texas. In the beginning, cotton was the important industry, and a gin operated as early as 1825. When the town was incorporated in 1830, it was the closest port city to New Orleans and served as an entry point for immigrants arriving both over land and by sea. Later, men from Matagorda were among those who signed the Goliad Declaration of Independence. Matagorda became the county seat in 1837, and by 1838, the community published a newspaper, and hotels were open for business. But the community was plagued by hurricanes, and by 1950 the population in Matagorda plummeted to only 650 people.

Today Matagorda offers twenty-two-plus miles of sandy shores, the warm waters of the Gulf of Mexico, and some of the finest saltwater fishing on the Gulf Coast. The historic town of Matagorda is in the center of the coastline on the Colorado River.

ADVENTURES IN HISTORY

One thing Stephen F. Austin should have remembered when he sent founders Elias Wightman, Hosea League, and Ira Ingram to Matagorda as proprietors, is history and the disaster of 140 years ago when LaSalle established Fort St. Louis right across the bay. Those colonists lost out to the lashings of numerous storms that buffeted the area all too frequently. In 1829, things started out well for Wightman and friends. Several dozen passengers sailed the first ship to reach Matagorda. However the trip, which was to have taken seven days, took thirty-one days. The colony failed, but by 1834 about 1,500 people made the town their home. After the Civil War, farmers turned to cattle raising, and a burgeoning beef industry was born.

But nature continued to plague the area, and constant hurricanes besieged the town. In the twenty-year period ending in 1891, Matagorda was hit nine times by either hurricanes or tropical storms. In 1894 the county seat was changed from Matagorda to Bay City. Although some businesses flourished, like the production of road-building material and chicken feed, fish and oysters became the major local business. The population in 1942 was reported as 1,250, by 1950 it had declined to 650; however, the summer influx of visitors swells that number considerably. Hurricanes, such as Carla in 1961, although lessened by the construction of a protective levee around the town, still took a toll on the community.

All that's left today is a post office, some churches, an elementary school, and a few shops. Even though Matagorda is not what Austin envisioned as a great seaport, it hasn't become a ghost town either. Far from being a lonely deserted place, Matagorda is now a favorite fisherman's getaway. It's an area for people to enjoy the river and broad beach or even feel a sense of history as they cast a line, glance at the sky, and remember the storms that destroyed Austin's dream of a seaport but gave folks a town to enjoy.

ON THE MAP

Located at the end of Highway 60 South, the town is seven miles by car from the Gulf of Mexico. Matagorda is near the Colorado River mouth and a two-hour drive from Houston.

WEEKEND ADVENTURES

The Matagorda County Museum in Bay City has early clothing, books, Texas maps, century-old carpentry tool collections, late seventeenth-century music, and archives. After a visit to the museum, stop by the Matagorda County Birding Nature Center that spans 34 acres. Otherwise, enjoy the near-natural state of this barrier island. Matagorda Island State Park stretches nearly 38 miles southwest from Pass Cavallo, near Port O'Connor, to the Aransas National Wildlife Refuge.

BEST TIME TO VISIT

When the fish are biting, sit back and enjoy. Or visit in October each year when the town puts on Matagorda Day with a parade of hand decorated vehicles, horseback riders, and booths selling food and gifts.

ADVENTURES IN LODGING AND DINING

If you're going to combine fishing with your historical sightseeing, do hang your hat at the Full Stringer Lodge overlooking the Colorado River and West Matagorda Bay. They've provided good food and lodging for over forty years. Other accommodations can be made at the Matagorda Dunes Condos or the Mayhew Manor, a bed and breakfast with home-cooked breakfasts. RV parks and the Matagorda Shell Shoppe Motel are also available.

For what is known as the best in fresh fish and seafood caught on Matagorda Bay or the Gulf of Mexico, take your taste buds to Captain Buddy's ship, the *Elaine Marie*. Look for the orange sign. Matagorda's newest restaurant, the Waterfront Restaurant, advertises "Where you come for the food and stay for the view!"

FOR MORE INFORMATION

Visit the Matagorda website www.matagordatexas.com.

THE WIDOW'S TALE

——— PORT LAVACA ———

Located on a bluff about fifteen to twenty feet above Lavaca Bay, Port Lavaca was founded after the Comanche attack on Linnville in 1840. Many who lost their homes in the raid envisioned the Lavaca area as an important shipping point and established new homesteads in the settlement. How fitting that a town named Lavaca, "the cow," should prosper as a hub of cattle and shipping. Eventually Lavaca became the busiest port on Matagorda and Lavaca Bays during the Republic of Texas period.

When Calhoun County was established, Lavaca became the county seat. After the end of the Civil War, it lost the county seat to Indianola. The two towns played this swapping game many times until the hurricane of 1886 wiped out Indianola and that town was abandoned. Even when Lavaca had lost the Morgan Lines to Indianola, Lavaca continued to prosper, exporting cattle, hides, tallow, and horns as well as many other items. In the late 1800s, Lavaca took on the name Port Lavaca. As time went on, exports changed from cattle and cattle-related items to seafood, and the export of shrimp became a major industry. As Port Lavaca became known for its fishing and hunting, tourism assumed a greater importance to the town's economy.

ADVENTURES IN HISTORY

Major Hugh Oran Watts's grave is in Port Lavaca, but the cause of his death seems to depend on who tells the tale. When the Comanches reached the tiny port of Linnville, in August of 1840, one of the men killed was the collector of customs, Major Watts. A large war party had descended on the tiny town. Warriors broke into the customs office, killed Watts, and grabbed his wife, Juliet. The Comanches were diverted from their course of action when they tried to strip the woman. Frustrated by the whalebone corset the Major's wife wore, they left her in her underwear and tied her to a pony. In the meantime, the rest of the residents ran to shore and escaped in boats.

But that's not the only version of the story. Yes, the Comanches tried to kill everyone in the small town, but they all managed to get to the boats. However, Watts's wife, a new bride, discovered she'd forgotten her favorite gold watch. She implored her husband to return to the town with her. When he agreed, they went ashore. He was tomahawked, and she was taken prisoner. When the Comanches tried to kill Mrs. Watts with an arrow, the steel stays in her corset deflected it. Stymied, the Comanches took her prisoner until the posse caught up with them and freed her. Whatever the story, the outcome's the same: Mrs. Watts's corset saved her life. She later remarried and became an outstanding member of the community in Lavaca.

On the Map

Port Lavaca is located about 30 miles southeast of Victoria and about 95 miles from Corpus Christi. For San Antonio residents, it's a day's trip; for Houston residents, a mere two-hour drive.

Weekend Adventures

According to Rita Miller, Interim Executive Director of the Port Lavaca, Calhoun County Chamber of Commerce & Agriculture, lighthouse enthusiasts love the two lighthouses in the area. The 1858 Halfmoon Reef Lighthouse, the oldest surviving wooden lighthouse structure in Texas, serves as a visitor's center in Port Lavaca. The 1857 Matagorda Island Lighthouse, located on the Gulf of Mexico barrier reef outside of Port O'Connor, is described as a challenging day trip.

The Indianola County Historic Park is the site of Old Indianola. The La Salle Monument, erected at the Indianola site, commemorates the spot where La Salle is thought to have first landed in 1685. For a guide to the more than thirty historical markers in Calhoun County, contact the Calhoun County Historical Commissions or the Chamber of Commerce. The Calhoun County Museum, a history museum, is focused on the towns of Port Lavaca and Indianola.

For an interesting stroll, head out to the 2,200-foot-long boardwalk, the Formosa Wetlands Walkway and a dedicated bird sanctuary, the world's longest boardwalk made from recycled plastic. It encircles federally protected wetland as well as providing access to the Alcoa Bird Tower.

Best Time to Visit

Along with a visit to the many historical sites in Port Lavaca, take advantage of the spring season to view the migration of birds along the roadsides. Birding lists and maps are available at the Chamber of Commerce.

Adventures in Lodging and Dining

Port Lavaca has a number of cabins and bed and breakfast places for visitors to stay. Try the Indianola House Bed & Breakfast where you'll dwell in part of a house built in Indianola in the 1840's and later shipped to Matagorda and refurbished. Relax in the backyard that faces the bay in Oldtown. Magnolia Cottage, which opened in June 2004, is also a good place to check out. Many cabins, bed and breakfasts, and motels in nearby Port O'Connor and Seadrift are also available.

The folks in Port Lavaca are very proud of their seafood restaurants. Captain Joe's, with its deck overlooking the Lavaca Bay, offers seafood with a Vietnamese flair. In addition, Barkett's in Seadrift has been serving mouth-watering seafood for over fifty years.

For More Information

Contact the Port Lavaca–Calhoun County Chamber of Commerce and Agriculture (www.portlavacainfo.com).

THE BOSTON HARBOR OF THE WEST

Velasco

Once the temporary capital of the Republic of Texas, Velasco is now the site of a pink granite marker proclaiming her past glory. Around 1821 the schooner *Lively* landed in Velasco with the first of Stephen F. Austin's colonists. Eventually Mexico set up a customs port there, and more than

25,000 settlers came through the port. The community of Old Velasco developed upstream from the coast becoming one of the oldest towns in Texas.

On June 26, 1832, the Texas colonists and Mexican troops fought the Battle of Velasco. A treaty of peace between Texas and Mexico was signed there in 1836, but Mexico never ratified the treaty. Although President Burnet made the town the temporary capital of the Republic of Texas, Velasco had its share of hardships, and a cholera epidemic reduced the population to one hundred in 1834. Mexico didn't recognize Texas independence until the U.S.–Mexican War ended in 1848. Between the Texas Revolution and the Civil War, Velasco blossomed as a summer resort for wealthy plantation families in the region. But, when the Civil War destroyed the plantation system, Velasco declined as a resort. Hardship continued to plague Velasco, and by 1884, there were only fifty residents, a general store, and a boat builder's shop.

Things turned around in 1891 when the new town of Velasco was surveyed and built about four miles upstream from the old town. Velasco rebuilt slowly, and in 1957, Velasco's four thousand people incorporated with Freeport, and the community became part of the Brazosport industrial and port area and the Brazosport Independent School District.

ADVENTURES IN HISTORY

In a news article reprinting of a pamphlet titled, *Sketch of the Life of Judge Edwin Waller*, mention is made of an eyewitness to the deeds of the Texas pioneers. The unknown witness claims unjust duties and taxes were the cause of the Texas rebellion against Mexico. Although taxation without representation was the rallying cry of the famous Tea Party in Boston Harbor, the plight of the Texans before the revolution that separated Texas from Mexico was remarkably similar to the Bostonians'. It is in this short clipping that Velasco is first called the Boston Harbor of the Texas Revolution. Both cried out against taxes and duties unjustly demanded by the government, and each is said to have caused a rebellion.

On the Map

Although Velasco was incorporated in 1957 with Freeport, the site of Fort Velasco has been found in Surfside Beach near City Hall. However, a portion is also located on the other side of the Freeport Channel within the town of Quintana. Freeport, located where the Brazos River meets the Texas Gulf Coast, is approximately 50 miles south of Houston. Quintana is located on the other side of the Freeport Channel from Surfside Beach.

Weekend Adventures

The Brazoria County Historical Museum is housed in the 1897 Brazoria County Courthouse. The Columbia Historical Museum traces the history of the area, and has an entire room devoted to a diorama of the town as founded in 1823. Columbia was the first capital of the Republic of Texas during the final months of 1836. In fact, the town is the home of the triple-trunk live oak tree known as the Independence Tree.

Historical driving tours can be found at local hotels and at the West Columbia Chamber of Commerce. The tour tape is narrated by popular author and news anchor, Ron Stone. A trip to the banks of Lake Jackson takes you to the Jackson Plantation Archeological Site. The Varner-Hogg Plantation State Historic Site is history-rich and a great place for sightseeing in the West Columbia area. The Lake Jackson Historical Museum features four eras of the area's development.

Sea Center Texas is a marine development, aquarium, and educational center that offers what they call "touch tanks." For a look at a true shrimp trawler, stop by the Shrimp Boat Monument on display at the head of the Brazosport Harbor. Also, plan a stop at Quintana Beach County Park to see the house-built-to-float, the Coveney House, now a museum, as well as other historical sites.

Best Time to Visit

Some folks like to visit the area the last weekend in July when the nearby town of Clute holds the annual Great Texas Mosquito Festival.

Adventures in Lodging and Dining

Try the Country Hearth Inn in Freeport and the Anchor Motel in Surfside. Quintana Beach County Park with its old-fashioned style cabins also offers full RV hookups as well as tent camping. Food is abundant in all the areas. Watch the boats go by at Dan's Water Front in Surfside where the menu offers steak, seafood, and an oyster bar.

For More Information

To contact the Brazosport Area Chamber of Commerce, e-mail Chamber@brazosport.org or visit the website at www.brazosport.org.

7

In and Around the Panhandle and West Texas

For most folks, when you say "West Texas," it means the vast terrain that stretches from the Big Bend Country to El Paso. When you add the vast area of the Panhandle, the region becomes vast and grand, indeed. Big Bend National Park is more than 801,000 acres and claims canyons, woodlands, and the Chihuahuan Desert. The countryside is equally diversified with the landscape changing from desert to mountains, waterfalls to canyons.

Ancient moments are forever captured in 4,000-year-old Indian pictographs, such as those in Seminole Canyon State Park near Del Rio. The area is a treasure trove for those with an archaeological bent. Four hundred archaeological sites make the area among the nation's richest in aboriginal cave paintings. They can be found in the Amistad National Recreation Area and the Seminole Canyon State Park and Historic Site near Langtry. A trip to El Paso can lead to a visit to the Hueco Tanks State Historic Site, natural rock basins, where, among the Indian pictographs, travelers can make out the names of intrepid Gold Rush forty-niners who stopped for water on their way to find their fortunes in California.

But West Texas has another face, that of the small towns and hole-in-the-wall cafes. Every March Texas cowboy poets gather in Alpine, Texas, for the Texas Cowboy Poetry Gathering, the second oldest cowboy gathering in the United States, held on the campus of Sul Ross State University. Langtry, near the Rio Grande, celebrates the infamous Hang'em High Judge Roy Bean. The Judge Roy Bean Visitor Center has a courtroom and billiard hall, a rustic saloon, even an opera house; but if you're looking for the good judge's gravesite, go to Del Rio's Whitehead Memorial Museum. The town of Terlingua, with an estimated population of two hundred and fifty, hosts about five thousand "chiliheads," who gather for the annual International Championship Chili Cookoff. And rock and roll enthusiasts pay homage to the late, great Roy Orbison with a visit to Wink's Roy Orbison Museum. Orbison grew up in Wink, Texas, and considered the small town his home.

Historic sites such as Fort Davis and Fort Stockton bring the past alive. The Fort Davis National Historic Site is operated by the National Park Service and includes both ruins and restorations. Fort Stockton re-creates a nineteenth-century parade with the competing sounds of hoofbeats and trumpeting bugles. The Historic Fort Stockton offers a glimpse into what life in a frontier fort was all about; and the Old Fort Cemetery provides stark evidence of the short lives of those who lived on the frontier. Travelers won't want to miss seeing Fort Stockton's Paisano Pete, the 20-foot long and 11-foot tall largest roadrunner in the world.

For a glimpse into recent history, a trip to the Midland-Odessa minimetroplex does the trick. While Crawford, Texas, claims to be Bush Country, Midland-Odessa proudly cries "George Bush Lived Here." Both father and son had homes in both towns. While the George W. Bush Childhood Home offers an intimate look at the 43rd president, Odessa's Presidential Museum has the unique claim of being the only museum in the United States dedicated solely to the office of the president. The museum includes the former home of President George H. W. Bush, but the father-son duo are not the only presidents that fall under the museum's microscope. Permanent exhibits focus on all aspects of presidents, including items relating to vice presidents, first ladies—even the also-rans, as well as presidents of the Republic of Texas and the Confederate States of Texas.

Although some folks are purists and consider West Texas, and the Panhandle separate areas, others group the two together. If West Texas is wide and big, the Panhandle plains are flat. But flat doesn't mean ugly or uninspiring. The renowned artist Georgia O'Keeffe drew inspiration from the Panhandle's Palo Duro Canyon area and called Texas her spiritual home. In addition to the usual Old West and cowboy history, the Panhandle also has a wonderful collection of oddities such as the public art on the Cadillac Ranch and the wee bit of Ireland in Shamrock, Texas, with a bit of the Blarney Stone. For devotees of Route 66, there's McLean's Devil's Rope and Route 66 Museum. Drop over to Lubbock's Mackenzie Park and check out a real live prairie dog town, and take a side-trip to Eastland to see the remains of Old Rip, the famous horned lizard. Rumor has it that Old Rip spent thirty-one years caught inside a courthouse cornerstone.

But don't think the Panhandle neglects its frontier forts. Fort Belknap, Fort Richardson, and Fort Griffin dot the landscape. Albany's annual Fandangle brings out the crowd for a re-enactment of the settling of Fort Griffin. Fort Concho, considered one of the best preserved frontier military outposts west of the Mississippi, puts a visit to San Angelo at the top of the list. A National Historic Landmark, Fort Concho brings the Buffalo Soldiers alive. The fort was their headquarters. Frontier medicine is brought to the forefront with the Robert Wood Johnson Museum of Frontier Medicine.

For a taste of amateur rodeo, go to Stamford's Texas Cowboy Reunion, billed as the greatest amateur rodeo in the world. Cowboy-lovers travel to the Red River Valley Museum in Vernon, Texas. The Panhandle-Plains Historical Museum, on the campus of West Texas A&M, recently finished a six-million-dollar renovation and offers a museum and a research center. The Pioneer Amphitheater in Palo Duro Canyon presents "TEXAS Legacies," the outdoor dramas that feature many of Texas's famous and infamous, and relates the story of the Great State. A pioneer schoolroom greets visitors at the Firehall Museum in Crowell, Texas. The Depot Library/Museum features Crowell's history and includes an extensive collection on Cynthia Ann Parker, the girl taken by the Indians and recaptured by white men in 1860. A trip to Paint Rock will result in an excursion to see the pictographs, and a visit to Pampa takes in the Revolutionary Way at the Freedom Museum USA. After learning about the impact of the railroad on the development of the state, go to Wichita Falls and visit the Railroad Museum, where you can see the old railcars, then stop in at the Wichita Falls Fire & Police Museum to see the turn-of-the-century fire-fighting equipment and old police motorcycles.

A trip to West Texas and the Panhandle today opens up the vast reservoir of Texas history.

YOU'RE A SPRAY PAINT CAN AWAY FROM ART

——— AMARILLO ———

Amarillo sits at the crossroads of America, almost equidistant from both coasts. Amarillo and the Texas Panhandle have been on the trip route of world travelers since the sixteenth century when Francisco Coronado arrived in 1541 and became the first European to see the American Southwest. From then on, a stream of cattlemen and sheepherders crossed the land in search of a better life.

Amarillo, a commercial site from the beginning, began as a place for Colorado merchants to put their stores. Originally named Oneida, the name was changed to Amarillo, meaning "yellow" in Spanish, after the yellow soil and yellow flowers found along the creekbed. Residents painted their houses yellow in honor of the new name. By the 1890s Amarillo had become a major cattle-shipping point, and with the added railroads, shipping and the population increased. While good for business, the Bowery District became notorious for its saloons, brothels, and desperadoes and increased in size and in crime. Prohibition later led to the demise of the District.

Today Amarillo showcases two lifestyles: the working ranches, unchanged from the nineteenth century, and the new twenty-first-century modern west. Amarillo has been home to celebrities such as Amarillo Slim and has been celebrated in song by George Strait in "Amarillo by Morning." Often called the gateway to Palo Duro Canyon, America's second largest canyon, the city might also be called a gateway to the Old West.

ADVENTURES IN HISTORY

Most folks have either heard of the Cadillac Ranch or seen the line of nose-first-into-the-ground Cadillacs gracing the Amarillo skyline. And most folks shake their heads and wonder why. For thirty years, the talk and the smiles have continued. A Cadillac, the grand dame icon of the automobile world, deserves a better end than a nose-plunge into Amarillo sod, say some. Why on earth would anyone want to stand a car on end and bury it in the plains of Texas, others say. Still others enjoy the upside-down, slightly twisted vision.

Stanley Marsh, a local helium tycoon, wanted a piece of art that would be created specifically for his ranch. A friend of "The Ant Farm," a San Francisco group of artists dedicated to experimental art, Marsh went to artists and sought their input. All agreed: It was to be a tribute to the Cadillac's tail fin. A status symbol, the fin was big and stood forty-two inches off the ground. The vision was big. Ten Cadillacs, upended with noses into the ground, facing west. The public art sculpture would be a testament to the Golden Age of the Automobile, and people would be encouraged to spray paint their own messages or art onto the automobile bodies. Marsh and the Ant Farm searched junkyards and bought Cadillacs. Slinging sledgehammers, they smashed the front ends of the ten cars; then, in the wheat field, the group directed a backhoe operator to dig the holes and drop the cars. Since then thousands have visited the Cadillac Ranch.

So the next time a creative urge strikes, grab a spray paint can and head for the Cadillac Ranch.

On the Map

Amarillo sits in the center of the Panhandle and is located on Interstate 40. Cadillac Ranch can be found west of Amarillo on Interstate 40, between exits 60 and 62.

Weekend Adventures

Amarillo has any number of historical sites and attractions. The American Quarter Horse Heritage Center and Museum details the colorful history of this animal. A drive down Historic Route 66 offers a nostalgic look at America and includes the Cadillac Ranch. History buffs should take in the Panhandle-Plains Historical Museum. To experience the cowboy life, check out Silver Mesa Ranch's horseback rides, horse-drawn wagons, cowboy breakfasts or dinners, Old West gunfights, and more. To see a herd of bison grazing on a range, go to the Amarillo Zoo.

Best Time to Visit

The Tri-State Fair draws thousands of visitors every September. Many visitors like to come in the summer to time their trips with *Lone Star Rising*. This musical production about the cultural history of the Lone Star State and Texas legacies is the epic outdoor theater production by the Texas Panhandle Heritage Foundation.

Adventures in Lodging and Dining

Most of the hotels and motels are found along Interstate 40. For Old West décor, try The Big Texan Hotel. The Ambassador Hotel is the city's finest, and there are a number of Best Western Inns. There are plenty of restaurants but none known as well as the Big Texan Steak Ranch, Opry, and Cowboy Palace. Known around the world for its 72-oz. steak dinner with all the trimmings including appetizer, salad, and potato, the restaurant issues a challenge. The meal, if eaten in one hour, is free. For something different, try the Cowboy Morning Breakfast and the Cowboy Evening Dinner. They'll do the cooking, but you'll do the living as you sit around the campfire and enjoy the good eats.

FOR MORE INFORMATION

Contact the Amarillo Convention Bureau and Visitors Center (www.visitamarillotx.com). For more detailed information on the Cadillac Ranch, go online to www.libertysoftware.be/cml/cadillac ranch/crmain.htm.

LIQUID GOLD

──── BIG BEND NATIONAL PARK ────

"Big Bend is where water runs uphill, where rainbows wait for rain, and where the river lives in a stone box," states an old Indian legend that captures the beauty and wildness of a legendary and timeless area. The Rio Grande River bends and curves, forming a big bend along the Texas and Mexico border that provides the name for the area. Established in 1944 with a total of 1,250 square miles, Big Bend National Park ranks with Yosemite and Grand Canyon as one of the largest parks in the continental United States. The area is a natural wonder, a place that continues to evolve in both land and people. Evidence of humans dates back to the Archaic or Desert Culture, and the red cinnabar cave paintings on the walls and entrances stand testament to their existence. By 1200 AD, the cultures had evolved to agricultural societies such as the La Junta people. During the 1500s, Spaniards came through the area in their search for gold, silver, and fertile lands, and enslaved the Chiso Indians to work the Spanish mines.

The 1700s brought the Apaches, and in the nineteenth century, the Comanches swept through and raided the Mexican settlers. After the

Mexican War of 1848, the Texans cast their eyes on the region. Major changes occurred after gold was discovered in California, and military forts appeared along the route that passed through the Big Bend area. Survey parties, beginning in 1852 with the Emory party, explored the river and the locale. After 1920, both Mexican settlers and Anglo-Americans farmed the land and raised cotton and food even after Big Bend National Park was established in 1944. But Big Bend isn't prized only for its beauty or farmland. The flowers give Big Bend its colorful landscape, and they also play an important role in the economy.

Adventures in History

Although Big Bend is America's least visited park, it ranks high in historic sites. Mention Big Bend, and the Rio Grande River comes quickly to mind. Years ago, in a popular legend of the day, Pecos Bill took a stick and dug the Rio Grande. His plow stuck and bent because he made a U-turn in southwest Texas and created Big Bend. Follow Pecos Bill to Presidio and see the great river rush toward the canyon walls of Big Bend National Park. The first national park in Texas is the size of Rhode Island and is a land where opposites reside. Heat and drought give way to cold and floods, arid lowland becomes moist mountain woodland, and a river coexists with the desert.

With three different ecological areas, river, desert, and mountain, Big Bend is home to a large variety of plants. One of those plants grown in the Chihuahuan Desert sector is known as the candelilla or little candle plant. Although full of pretty flowers, Candelilla's bronze-looking stems are what command attention. During the rainy season, the stems fill with a thick sap that, in the dry season, coats the stem as a wax and prevents evaporation. Retired army captain C. D. Wood knew all about the candelilla wax, sometimes known as liquid gold. Knowing how much the army valued the plant's waterproofing ability, Captain Wood built a candelilla wax–producing factory. Harvesting the wax proved to be hard work, even more so since it was done in the desert. Wax workers received the equivalent of one dollar a day for their labor. Eventually, wax making became Big Bend's third largest industry after ranching and mining. Today candellila is used as a thickening agent and emollient in products such as lipstick to give them form.

On the Map

Three paved roads lead to the park. U.S. 385 from Marathon, Texas, leads to the north entrance. State Route 118 from Alpine, Texas, accesses the west entrance. Ranch Road 170 from Presidio to Study Butte, and then State Route 118 goes to the west entrance. Big Bend National Park headquarters is located 70 miles south of Marathon, Texas, and 108 miles from Alpine, Texas, via Highway 118.

Weekend Adventures

Big Bend offers many tourist activities. For history buffs, a trip to the Museum of the Big Bend at Sul Ross State University is a treat. The park is rich in cultural history and archeological sites. Journey back in time with a visit to an area where two cultures mixed, the Castolon Historic District, listed in the National Register of Historic Places. Castolon lays claim to the oldest adobe in Big Bend, the Alvino house. From mid-November to mid-April, volunteers present interpretive programs, guided walks, auto caravans, and evening programs.

Best Time to Visit

While the park is not very crowded much of the year, March and April are the busiest times, especially during spring break. Major holidays, such as Easter and Thanksgiving weekends, and the week between Christmas and New Year's Day are also packed, with all lodging and campsites usually full. If you prefer an uncrowded atmosphere, try visiting in August and September.

ADVENTURES IN LODGING AND DINING

The Chisos Mountains Lodge, tucked into the peace and serenity of the Chisos Mountains, is the only lodge in the park. However, there is plenty of lodging in the near vicinity. The Badlands Hotel with western décor and its own paleontologist, and the Wilson House Historic Hotel, built in 1920 and fully renovated in 1978, offer visitors a glimpse of history. The Chisos Mountains Lodge Restaurant in the Chisos Basin with its spectacular view offers Tex-Mex food. Nearby, any number of cafes, restaurants, and diners in Alpine are happy to greet travelers.

FOR MORE INFORMATION

The Big Bend National Park website (www.nps.gov/bibe/home.htm.) presents plenty of suggestions. Another source of information is the Brewster Counter Tourism Council (www.visitbigbend.com).

WHEN THE EARL CAME TO STAY

——— BIG SPRING ———

In times past, anyone making his way through the dusty Panhandle of West Texas considered himself lucky to come upon the ancient big spring in Sulphur, Texas. The spring is known as a watering place for various wild animals, such as coyotes, wolves, and mustangs. Although a trouble spot when both the Comanche and Shawnee Indians claimed the right to water at the spring, it was also a campsite used by early expeditions trekking across this area of West Texas. In the late 1870s the community of Big Spring was nothing more than some hide huts and saloons in a wild and woolly town. However, in 1880 the Texas and Pacific Railroad passed by the town, hauling in all sorts of materials, and left with cattle and buffalo bones. Because of the trains, the small community decided to move nearer the tracks, resulting in the development of railroad shops as well as a railway station. Eventually the town grew and became the Howard County seat. With the discovery of oil, the city experienced the typical growth and decline pattern that happened all over Texas when an area struck oil. World War II brought the Big Spring Army Corps Bombardier School. In the 1950s, with a renewed military presence at Webb Air Force Base and thriving banking and petrochemical industries, the city came into its own with county fairs and rodeos. Music flowed and honky-tonks promoted many future famous performers.

Today, Big Spring has moved comfortably into the twenty-first century with its hospitals, prisons, and other public sector institutions. Blessed with high employment and a low cost of living, this picturesque city with its namesake landmark is a constant draw for residential living and visitors alike.

ADVENTURES IN HISTORY

Mention Big Spring, Texas, and the last thing that might pop into anyone's mind would be an English earl. According to legend, marital difficulties plagued Joseph Heneage Finch, the Seventh Earl of Aylesford. Rumors of footprints in the snow leading to his wife's bedroom window drove the earl to seek refuge in the remotest region of the world he could find: Big Spring, Texas. The townsfolk didn't think much of his title, but they loved his generosity. He was known for picking up the tab at the town's drinking fests. Many legends about the earl are probably embellished, and may not be true; but one thing's for sure, they're certainly entertaining.

One such tale is rooted in Finch's preference for eating sheep. In cattle country, mutton wasn't the big item on the menu. So the earl not only brought his own butcher with him, he also opened his own shop. The first masonry building in Big Spring, the shop can still be seen today.

The earl clearly lived and played hard. Witnesses talk about mounds of whiskey and beer bottles at his ranch piled as tall as a haystack, and they counted three whiskey bottles for each bottle of beer. He also had the typical British penchant for understatement. Playing cards one evening, he got up from the table, said "Goodbye, Boys," and meant it literally. He left, went up to his room, climbed into bed—and died. A local doctor, preparing the earl for the return trip to England after his death, described his liver as being like a rock. When he died, he was only 36 years old.

On the Map

Big Spring is located at the intersection of Interstate 20 and U.S. Highways 80 and 87, State Highway 350, Farm Road 700, and the Missouri Pacific line in southwest central Howard County, about 39 miles northeast of Midland.

Weekend Adventures

Most travelers make their way to City Park to see the spring that gave the town its name. The 400-acre park also includes the Comanche Trail Amphitheater. Heritage walking tours take in the Railroad and Train Display and twenty-six historic buildings. Many take a tour of the Hanger 25 Air Museum, the site of Big Spring's WWII Army Air Corps Bombardier School and Webb Air Force Base. The Heritage Museum displays local and early West Texas history and houses the world's largest collection of Texas longhorn steer horns. There's a rare collection of phonographs made by Thomas Edison, Victor, Columbia, and others from the 1800s to 1920s. For architecture buffs, there's Howard County Courthouse, and the Settles Hotel. The Potton House is a showcase of Victorian life and architecture. Built around 1901 of red sandstone, the house has vintage furnishings as well and is listed in the National Register of Historic Places.

Best Time to Visit

Since one of the area's most interesting places to visit is Big Spring State Park, springtime would be a good time to enjoy the beauty of the nature trail. Or arrive anytime from late October to April and watch the sandhill cranes at the Sandhill Sanctuary, north of the State Park. While there, take in Comanche Trail Park right next door for its birding opportunities.

ADVENTURES IN LODGING AND DINING

Big Spring State Park has overnight camping facilities. Looking for a place to stay for a night, a week, or more? Try Annie's Bed & Breakfast on Highway 155 North in Big Sandy. Other area motels and inns include the Mayo Ranch Motel, Best Western Motor Lodge, and the Classic Inn, all in Big Spring.

For an assortment of eateries to ease those hunger pangs, try Herman's Restaurant for their specialty chicken fried steak; the Red Mesa Grill, where the Sonora Strip is a recommended dish, and the hot food is served piping hot; or Rocky's, a family owned restaurant known for excellent service as well as good food.

FOR MORE INFORMATION

To find out more about Big Spring, contact the Big Spring Chamber of Commerce (www.bigspringtx.com). For information about the Sandhill Sanctuary, call 915-263-4931.

THE EVOLUTION OF A TOWN

——— BUFFALO GAP ———

More than one hundred years ago Indians hunted the great herds of buffalo that roamed across West Texas. Located at a natural pass in the Callahan Divide, the town of Buffalo Gap had a total population of 493 in the year 2000. Once the county seat of Taylor County, Buffalo Gap Historic Village is now the major attraction. The up and down economy and population took its toll on the town's growth, but today the town tempts tourists with old-world charm and curiosity.

The town that took the county seat away from Buffalo Gap in a somewhat controversial manner is Abilene. The Texas and Pacific Railroad made the decision to go through Abilene, and from then on the cow town became the future great city of West Texas. A rowdy frontier town, Abilene still says it is the friendly frontier, but has transformed from the classic cow town into a modern city that offers rich history and friendly hospitality and has remained friendly with its former rival, Buffalo Gap.

Adventures in History

Buffalo Gap earned its name for the huge herds of buffalo that flowed through the gap on the way to the plains. By the 1870s the hide hunters and the cattlemen had arrived. The population grew, and before long Taylor County had its first town. Buffalo Gap had arrived. The town quickly became the seat of Taylor County and a courthouse and jail soon followed. By 1875 buffalo hunting proved to be a favorite sport. A carcass could get a man five to fifteen dollars and the bones, used to refine sugar, could be sold as well. Over time the railroads moved west, stretching across the state, and the Indians and the buffalo faded from view.

By the mid-1880s, Buffalo Gap claimed to be the Athens of the West, and the town didn't appear to have anything standing in its way. What the town didn't know was that a group of Abilene businessmen had approached the Texas and Pacific Railroad in order to lure the railroad away from Buffalo Gap to flatter, easier land. With high hopes for what they planned to be the future great city of the West, the railroad agreed to bypass Buffalo Gap and the town of Abilene, named for Abilene, Kansas, had managed a coup.

As if that weren't enough, the fine new citizens of Abilene decided their city should be the county seat, so they petitioned to have an election. Despite the strong efforts of the folks at Buffalo Gap, they lost the election. Buffalo Gap exerted great pressure and charged foul play. Railroad passengers passing through Abilene had voted illegally in favor of the new city. Abilene denied the charges. After much legal wrangling, Abilene took over as the county seat.

Over the years Buffalo Gap has earned the reputation of being an old-time cultural and commercial center. The Buffalo Gap Historic Village became a reality in 1956 when Ernest Wilson bought the courthouse and turned it into a museum of western and Indian artifacts. The museum owners continued to purchase more and more structures. In 1999 the Grady McWhiney Research Foundation, with help from the Taylor County Historical Society, bought the village and currently maintains the attraction as a non-profit educational facility. Today Buffalo Gap Historic Village continues to bring the Old West alive and provides a different weekend escape experience.

On the Map

Located in the northeast corner of Taylor County, Abilene is easily accessible by four major highways: Interstate 20, Highway 84 East/West, and Highways 83 and 277 North/South. From Abilene, take Buffalo Gap Road (FM 89) south for about fourteen miles to visit the town of Buffalo Gap.

Weekend Adventures

After you visit the Buffalo Gap Historic Village, further stops might include the antique shops in the commercial district located off Highway 89. The town is also home to a major flea market that occurs on the third weekend of the month in Old Settler's Reunion Ground. Nearby Abilene State Park has a refectory and an adjacent swimming pool. The refectory or pavilion is made of native red sandstone and sits on top of the park's highest hill, providing a panoramic view of the area.

Want more Texas history? Follow the Texas Forts Trail to visit these outposts: Fort Phantom, Fort Griffin, Fort Chadbourne, and Fort Concho. All have periodic living history events. A trip to Abilene takes you to the latest attraction: Frontier Texas! The center opened in 2004 and features buffalo hunting, a key to Buffalo Gap's past. The Grace Museum offers more West Texas history. For an interesting side trip, go to the nearby National for Center Children's Illustrated Literature.

BEST TIME TO VISIT

If you want to add a western-themed event to your trip, Abilene's West Texas Fair and Rodeo in September or the Western Heritage Classic in May might be the right ticket.

ADVENTURES IN LODGING AND DINING

Travelers have a range of lodgings available including the Hampton Inn Abilene, Ramada Inn, Day's Inn, and Comfort Inn. The Buffalo Gap Bed and Breakfast allows visitors to stay within two miles of the historic village. Many travelers like to stop at a converted hay barn known as the Perini Steakhouse. Located in Buffalo Gap, the restaurant is famed for offering a taste of mesquite-grilled steaks and other chuck-wagon cuisine.

FOR MORE INFORMATION

Online information for Abilene, Texas, is found at www.abilene.com. The McWhiney Foundation's online site provides information on the Buffalo Gap Historic Village (www.mcwhiney.org/buffgap/bghome.html).

A FIRE SWEPT THROUGH

HISTORIC FORT BLISS

Fort Bliss lies outside downtown El Paso. In 1998, Fort Bliss celebrated its 150th anniversary. The celebration led to more tourism as Fort Bliss made its historic sites more accessible to the public. Dozens of buildings and homes from the 1800s to the early 1900s became known as Historic Fort Bliss.

First established in 1849 and known as the post opposite El Paso, the fort went through four sites before moving to its current location in 1893. Infantry and cavalry troops known as the "U.S. Colored Troops" were garrisoned there from 1866. Many of the original structures from 1893 are still in use. Today Fort Bliss is the home of the United States Army Air Defense Artillery Center and School and all FORSCAM Air Defense Artillery Brigades.

The history of Fort Bliss is peppered with the appearance of many larger-than-life figures including Buffalo Bill Cody, Pancho Villa, George S. Patton, Jr., and John J. "Black Jack" Pershing. During 1916–1917, Fort Bliss became known as the mobilization point for Black Jack Pershing's Punitive Expedition into Mexico.

Adventures in History

General John J. Pershing, quartermaster of the famed Buffalo Soldiers, the U.S. 10th Cavalry, was not without his share of troubles. As 1st Lieutenant, Pershing met with disaster early on when he and his troops left for Cuba on the *Leona*, a coastal merchant ship. Not only did the *Leona* become separated from its convoy, the troops became seasick, hungry, and lived in bad conditions. Trouble continued when they finally arrived at Daiquiri. The port didn't have adequate facilities, so small boats had to be used. The men, carrying their equipment, ended up jumping from the boats and wading to shore. Two men drowned. Problems continued. Pershing had to push forward toward Santiago despite a lack of supplies, malaria, and yellow fever. In spite of all the hardships Pershing and his men faced, the United States prevailed and won Santiago. Pershing and his men had waged a successful campaign.

Pershing's worst days occurred at Fort Bliss. On August 17, 1915, Pershing began his day like any other. At the time he lived alone in Quarters No 1. His wife and four children were still in California at the Presidio of San Francisco. His wife had been in a carriage accident and had back injuries. Pershing looked forward to being reunited with his family. While he attended to his morning duties, the phone rang. The voice on the other end gave him the shock of his life when he was informed that a fire had swept through his quarters in San Francisco. A few minutes later, his aide gave him a telegram saying his wife and three daughters had died in the fire. Only his six-year-old son survived.

Pershing went on to have a varied and successful military career. In 1916 Francisco (Pancho) Villa attacked Columbus, New Mexico, and Pershing was directed to lead the Punitive Division in their efforts to capture Villa. Fort Bliss became the main supply base. During that time, Pershing introduced aerial reconnaissance in an effort to discover the best way into the terrain. Although he never did capture Villa, the effort scattered Villa's men. Pershing returned to Fort Bliss in 1917. He went on to serve in World War I and helped frame the Treaty of Versailles. In 1919 he achieved the rank of General of the Armies of the United States. He died in 1948.

Today, Quarters No. 1 still sits at the corner of Sheridan and Chaffee roads among all the other historic buildings that make up Historic Fort Bliss. Built in 1910, the house is an architectural mix of New Colonial and part California adobe. At some point, Quarters No. 1 became the Pershing House. The home, although still in use by the Army, is considered a shrine to General Pershing.

On the Map

Fort Bliss is located in El Paso north of Interstate 10 and east of U.S. 54. At the gate, guards check your driver's license, auto liability insurance, and inspection sticker.

Weekend Adventures

Travel El Paso's Mission Trail to see three active missions, including the oldest mission in Texas, Ysleta, founded in 1682, and San Elizario, established in 1789—one of the best preserved. Museum rich, El Paso has a list of museums that include the El Paso Museum of History, the Border Patrol Museum, and the new Tigua Cultural Center near the Ysleta mission. Military historians will enjoy the War Eagles Museum. Be sure to stop by the boot hill cemetery, the historic Concordia, where the infamous gunfighter John Wesley Hardin is buried.

BEST TIME TO VISIT

Fort Bliss celebrates Armed Forces Day weekend every year. The ten-day El Paso Heritage Festival in April is another good time to visit the area. Twice a year the Trinity Site Tour takes visitors to the White Sands Missile Range, the site of the first atomic bomb explosion. The annual Fort Selden Frontier Days is in April.

ADVENTURES IN LODGING AND DINING

With more than 7,000 lodgings, finding an inn is not a problem in El Paso. The Camino Real is listed on the National Historic Register, and the Tiffany glass dome is the showcase of the Dome Bar. The Bowen Ranch is a historic working cattle ranch with a view of the mountains and guest services. For plenty of fun and good dining, plan a visit to the Indian Cliffs Ranch at Cattleman's Steakhouse. Go early, see the sights and stay for dinner.

FOR MORE INFORMATION

To confirm information or events regarding Fort Bliss, contact the Fort Bliss Public Affairs Office (www.bliss.army.mil). For information on El Paso, contact the El Paso Visitors Convention and Visitors Bureau at www.elpasocvb.com. For a complete listing of El Paso area events, go to www.epscene.com.

BY GEORGE! LAREDO CELEBRATES WASHINGTON'S BIRTHDAY

LAREDO

Laredo, long considered the gateway to Mexico, has much to offer visitors. When many people hear the name Laredo, the tune and lyrics of the song "Streets of Laredo" come to mind: "As I walked out on the streets of Laredo." Written in 1876 by Francis Henry Maynard, the song evokes images of gunfights on street corners and bodies in boot hill cemeteries. Still others think of Larry McMurtry's film or book by the same name. While those days have gone the way of the historic Old West, Laredo's past is present at every turn.

Laredo and history go hand-in-hand. Founded on the north bank of the Rio Grande in 1755 by Captain Tomás Sánchez and three other families, the city wasn't laid out until 1767. Cowboys drove cattle along the San Antonio–Laredo road to Saltillo. Under the Treaty of Guadalupe Hidalgo in 1848, Laredo became an official part of Texas.

Today Laredo is a bustling city. Sister cities Laredo and Nuevo Laredo are connected by the International Bridge, making Laredo a major port of entry into Mexico and the second fastest growing city in the United States. Visitors can take the two-hour Heritage Tour on the turn-of-the century trolley. Laredo is a shopper's heaven, and travelers will find plenty of opportunities as trade flows freely between the sister cities. Laredo also puts on South Texas's largest festival, Washington's Birthday Celebration. For more than one hundred years, this annual celebration has grown, improved, and evolved into the current two-week celebration that brings the city out and the travelers in.

ADVENTURES IN HISTORY

When people hear of Laredo's George Washington Birthday Celebration, they ask, "Why would a town so far removed from the Revolutionary War and the early colonial days of the United States be celebrating George Washington's birthday?" The people of Laredo are proud to put on this two-week international fiesta, the largest and longest tribute to the nation's first president, and the tradition goes way back.

In 1898 the original planners of the celebration were looking for a traditionally American holiday, one that would allow them to celebrate the best of all cultures influencing the heritage of Laredo. The planners were all members of the Improved Order of the Red Men, local chapter Yaqui Tribe #59, and included Laredoans of Mexican and American ancestry. The knew of the Sons of Liberty and their fight for freedom, and they knew the Sons of Liberty would often disguise themselves as Indians in order to meet and discuss their strategy. They also knew that during the early days of the Revolution, George Washington took the name of Sachem as his code name. Finally, they learned that the same Washington had been revered and respected as the forerunner of liberators such as Father Hidalgo and Simon Bolivar. In the person of Washington, the people of Laredo found everything they needed to bring their tradition alive.

On February 22, 1898, the townspeople held a mock battle between the Indians and the white men for control of the city. The defenders fell, and the mayor presented the key to the city to the Great Chief Sachem who then presented the key to Princess Pocahontas, who represented lost tradition and a vanishing race. The first celebration lasted two days. A re-enactment of the Boston Tea Party was the final act. This two-day event became the beginning of what is now a two-week celebration commemorating George Washington's birthday.

Today the celebration is an institution that is not only uniquely Laredo, but also the largest and longest tribute to George Washington. Under the umbrella of fun, fiestas, and festivities, the celebration includes a carnival, fireworks display, a Jalapeño Festival, a Victorian Street Party, and the Jam for George. The Society of Martha Washington and the Princess Pocohantas Council host pageants and balls such as the Princess Pocohantas Pageant and Ball and the Society of Martha Washington Colonial Ball. Attendees are transported to the past with the presentation of the First Couple, George and Martha Washington, in a setting right out of the pages of the Revolutionary War. No expense is spared for these annual functions. Each year a hard-backed book, thick with pages and filled with photographs of women in extravagant period gowns, debutantes, and other participants is produced. The result resembles a very sophisticated yearbook. For Laredoans, George Washington's Birthday is "the" event of the year. During the International Bridge Ceremony, officials and dignitaries from Mexico and the United States exchange "abrazos" or hugs, and a parade follows. The two-week festival has become known as the celebration with something for everyone.

On the Map

The city is located on the United States/Mexico border, 150 miles from San Antonio and 150 miles north of Monterrey, Mexico.

Weekend Adventures

If you love architecture, be sure to visit the Webb County Courthouse, and then take a walk through the historic districts. History buffs will enjoy the Rio Grande Museum and the San Agustin Church, which is the oldest landmark in the city. Shoppers will want to go to Zaragosa Street and Avenida Guerrero. For cultural immersion try the Nuevo Mercado, New Market, but be prepared to bargain.

Best Time to Visit

Naturally, the two-week celebration is an ideal time to visit Laredo but any time is a good time to visit the gateway to Mexico.

Adventures in Lodging and Dining

La Posada Hotel Suites is said to be the undisputed grand dame of borderland hostelry on both sides of the Rio Grande and is located in the heart of the San Agustin Historical District. The La Quinta Inn Laredo is near the banks of the Rio Grande. For an extra dining treat, try the fajitas at the El Dorado Bar in Nuevo Laredo.

FOR MORE INFORMATION

Contact the Laredo Convention and Visitors Bureau (www.visit laredo.com) or the official city of Laredo website at www.ci.laredo .tx.us/.

LUBBOCK'S MANY WHATSITS

—— LUBBOCK ——

The area had been described as a treeless, desolate waste of uninhabited solitude, but early Texas farmers and ranchers didn't let that stop them. Two groups of settlers, one led by Frank E. Wheelock and the other by W. E. Rayner, moved into this area known as the High Plains of Texas and founded two settlements, Old Lubbock and Monterey. By the fall of 1890, the two groups decided to join together. They crafted an agreement, and the town of Lubbock was born. Four years later the town had a post office. But Lubbock remained small and indistinguishable until the railroad came to town. Lubbock then became a city.

Today Lubbock is thoroughly modern. Texas Technological College took up residence and added a medical school that became Texas Tech University Health Sciences Center. The city prospered. Then tragedy struck. A vicious tornado blew through the city and left twenty-six dead and $135 million in damages. But the citizens came together and rebuilt. Today the city is a thriving cultural and recreational center.

ADVENTURES IN HISTORY

For those who thought Marfa, Texas, had an exclusive claim on all the strange and eerie light sightings in Texas, think again. Throughout the sixties, seventies, and eighties, the local papers published accounts of Lubbock sightings. According to a report in the *Lubbock Avalanche Journal*, on August 31, 1951, Lubbock resident Carl Hart Jr. photographed unidentified flying objects in the night sky. Local residents confirmed the UFO sighting, but none could offer up any explanations.

Then there's the story of the Lubbock City Cemetery angel shedding tears. Talk was that if someone raced as fast as he could from the front gate to the angel statue, touching the statue's feet, the angel would shed tears. But the story of the fire on Halloween eve in 1950 that destroyed the seven-gabled house could be Lubbock's real mystery. Early town lore speaks of Gold Rush days when gold fever attacked nearly everyone, and a wagon train made its way across the Llano Estacado. As the wagon train neared the site of Lubbock, Indians attacked. All died, but not before the wagon train members buried their gold. Or so the story goes. Decades later a new family, the Rumphs, moved to town. The new family built a house outside of town, stayed to themselves, and were the object of small-town talk because of their propensity for digging around the house. Some residents said they saw lights in the basement. Several years later the family left. This set the town's gossips a-buzz with talks of maps and odd behavior. Did the family dig for gold? Did they find it? When the house burned later, the town revived their talk about the house and the wagon train, but locals continue to say the story is more lore than fact.

If you are intrigued and want to know more, plan a trip to Texas Tech's Southwest Collections/Special Collections Library where this story and more are chronicled. The town loves its stories and savors its lore and legends so much that the Visitors Center has named the online site www.lubbocklegends.com. A trip on the Internet will take you to a site called Halloween Lubbock Online (www.lubbockonline.com/halloween) where these stories are chronicled and where the lore of Lubbock's flames are fanned. So if you plan a trip in the fall, particularly during Halloween weekend, you just might want to see the production of Night of the Living Dead by the Lubbock Regional Arts Center, a Halloween Concert by the Texas Tech Orchestra, or take a visit to the haunted houses.

On the Map

Lubbock, the largest city in the South Plains, is approximately three hundred miles northwest of Dallas and one hundred miles south of Amarillo.

Weekend Adventures

Stop by the Buddy Holly Center, a historic landmark listed on the National Register of Historic Places. Holly fans will want to see the Buddy Holly statue and Walk of Fame on 8th and Avenue Q. The center is newly renovated, restored, and expanded and has a gallery, a Texas Musicians Hall of Fame, and a museum. The National Ranching Heritage Center, a museum and historical park, offers visitors a look at the ranching life. A new and interesting stop is the Silent Wings Museum, dedicated to glider flight. Texas Tech's Southwest Collections/Special Collections Library contains the Vietnam Archives, the largest collection of Vietnam materials outside the U.S. government's. The Lubbock Lake National Historic Landmark marks the spot where six-foot-long prehistoric armadillos and mammoths have been excavated. The interpretive center remains open year round.

Best Time to Visit

The Lubbock Arts Festival, a four-day celebration in April, has been a big happening for more than a quarter of the century. Other big celebrations include Las Fiestas Mexicanas and Juneteenth. For cowboy enthusiasts, check out the National Cowboy Symposium and Celebration held the week after Labor Day. Be sure to check the dates. In September look for the Panhandle–South Plains Fair.

Adventures in Lodging and Dining

The Dawkins House, circa 1929, is in Lubbock's South Overton National Historic District. There are plenty of accommodations in and around the city. Broadway Manor Bed and Breakfast is also in the historical district. Travelers won't have any trouble finding good food at the County Line Smokehouse and Grill where Texas hospitality and barbecue can be found in Escondido Canyon.

For More Information

Visit the Lubbock Convention and Visitors Bureau (www.lubbock legends.com).

The Glow of Mystery Lights

——— Marfa ———

Nestled between mountain ranges, the city of Marfa enjoys crisp, clear days and snuggles under a starlight canopy at night. Located 4,688 feet above sea level with a population of about 2,300 people, Marfa was established in 1881 as a water stop for the Texas and New Orleans Railroad.

Legend says the wife of the town's founder named the town Marfa from the Dostoyevsky novel, *Brothers Karamazov*. Known primarily for the mysterious Marfa lights, the town is also well known as the shooting location of the classic movie *Giant*, starring Rock Hudson, Elizabeth Taylor, Dennis Hopper, and James Dean. Marfa also serves as the gateway to the border towns of Mexico and to Big Bend National Park.

Adventures in History

They glow, they flow, they move and float. These are the strange ethereal lights of Marfa. They hang suspended in the air above the mountains with no discernable source or location. To observe these mysterious lights, travel about nine miles east of Marfa, Texas, wander at night around the base of the Chianti Mountains, and watch the sky. Are they a sleight of hand by an unseen magician? Perhaps they're an unsolved

conundrum like Big Foot or the Loch Ness Monster. Whatever is causing this phenomenon, it still remains a mystery. How and when the
lights of Marfa arrived has been a source of much speculation over the
years. According to the historical marker located at the Marfa Mystery
Lights viewing site, one of the first settlers in the area, Robert Ellison,
discovered the lights. Originally the lights were a Texas legend and story,
but they've long since captured the imagination and interest of the nation. Once thought to be nothing more than distant campfire lights,
now everyone has a theory, and there are as many theories as years that
have passed since the first discovery more than a century ago, in 1883.

Before Ellison found the lights, the Apache Indians believed they were
stars dropping to earth. Romantics suggest the ghostly lights are the torches
of dead lovers who roam the mountains and hunt endlessly through the
night in search of one another. Then there are those who consider them to
be St. Elmo's fire, ghostly blue flames that sailors believed were sent by their
patron saint to watch over them, or maybe they're just static electricity.
Whether swamp gas or, as pragmatists claim, car headlights moving down
nearby roads and highways, or high-pressure ranch lights, everyone has an
explanation for the source of the lights. The only problem with some of the
theories is that the lights have been in Marfa since before the dawn of electricity. According to the State of Texas road marker, "scholars have reported
over seventy-five local folk tales dealing with the unknown phenomenon."

Further mystifying matters is the appearance of the lights. Their
physical description varies, depending on whom you ask. Every year the
Marfa lights draw thousands of visitors from all over the world to this
small desert plain. To some, the lights are pure white and constantly
shining; although others say they're colorful and changeable. Some visitors have even reported up to ten lights hopping and skipping in the
desert air. While many have tried to study the phenomenon, all have left
thwarted because the lights disappear when approached. No one has
been able to get close enough to study them. So the lights remain unex-
plained, at least for now. There's only one thing everyone can agree on:
the mystery lights of Marfa do exist.

On the Map

Marfa is located on a Chihuahuan Desert plateau in the Trans-Pecos area of west Texas at the junction of U.S. Highways 97 and 67 in north-east Texas. In addition to driving, visitors can also use the Marfa Municipal Airport (MRF), located 5 miles north on Highway 17, or Amtrak or Greyhound.

Weekend Adventures

The new Marfa Mystery Lights Viewing Center extends across eight acres and features a viewing deck, and information about the Marfa lights and the general area. If you're a film history buff, visit the site of Reata from the movie *Giant* and Hotel Paisano, the movie's headquarters. The James Dean Memorial, now mostly ruins by the roadside on nearby Ryan Ranch, is still worth visiting.

Historical sites also include the Marfa and Presidio County Museum. Visit the museum for a glimpse of the region's history found in its collections of rare photographs and memorabilia. You might also want to take in the historic Humphris-Humphreys House and the Presidio County Courthouse. The Chinati Foundation Museum, a contemporary art museum, displays large-scale exhibitions and is located in converted buildings on a former military base, Fort D. A. Russell.

Best Time to Visit

To see the lights for yourself, take in the Marfa Lights Festival (www.marfalights.com) held on Labor Day, although, with Marfa's clear skies, temperate weather, and ideal atmosphere almost any time is a great time to visit. Be sure to remember that the ghostly lights are best seen at night. Many visit Marfa over Memorial Day Weekend. For a western theme, try Marfa in May for the Big Bend Hall of Fame Cowboy Rendezvous. Film buffs will mark their calendars for the Marfa July 4, 2005, celebration of the fiftieth anniversary of the movie *Giant*.

ADVENTURES IN LODGING AND DINING

Considered the most significant hotel between San Antonio and El Paso from the 1930s through the 1960s, the historic El Paisano Hotel offers plenty of amenities. For someplace different to stay, try the century-old Victorian adobe Arcon Inn, a bed and breakfast built in 1906 and brimming with colonial treasures. There are also many other bed and breakfasts in the area.

There are quite a number of restaurants in Marfa. Maiya's offers large portions and a changing menu of Italian cuisine, and Jett's Grill in the Paisano Hotel is known for its exceptional steaks and seafood.

FOR MORE INFORMATION

For further information on Marfa, Texas, go online to www.marfa lights.com or www.marfacc.com.

HOME OF THE WORLD'S FIRST RODEO

——— PECOS ———

Despite the time-honored phrase "West of the Pecos," the city of Pecos was once east of the river. The town now sits on the western bank of the Pecos River in the east central part of the state. Some say "pecos" means crooked and the river's crooked path gave the name to the town that began with a small plot of land and a depot. The town's name went from Pecos Station, to Pecos City, and then simply Pecos. Originally the county took its name from Pecos but changed to Reeves County in 1883.

Pecos is best known for the legend of Pecos Bill. The story goes that Bill, the youngest child of a Texas pioneer, was lost crossing the Pecos River. He survived because coyotes took him in and raised him. The boy believed he was a coyote until a cowboy found him and convinced him he was not a coyote but a human being. The cowboy also convinced Bill they were brothers. Pecos Bill quickly learned the cowboy trade and became known as the one who invented all the things ranchers needed to get the job done. Bill taught gophers to dig post holes and invented the cowboy song to calm cattle. Most folks know of his more famous exploits: roping wild longhorns with a rattlesnake rope, digging the Rio Grande with a stick, and, of course, riding a tornado.

Another near-mythic West Texas favorite associated with Pecos is the legendary Judge Roy Bean. Judge Bean presided over court in the town of Langtry, Texas. He called himself the "Law West of the Pecos," but his pet phrase, "Hang 'em first, try 'em later," earned him the moniker of the Hanging Judge. He was said to have kept a bear in his court. So many stories have grown up around the judge that separating the man from the myth is difficult, if not impossible.

At one time, things were pretty rough in the town of Pecos—so rough, in fact, that to "pecos" someone meant to ambush a man, steal his horse and money, kill him, and roll his body off down a riverbank. During its first year, the No. 11 Saloon even had a double-homicide. Things are much quieter now. The people are Texas-friendly, and travelers are more apt to run into cowboys competing for huge rodeo purses and Pecos residents offering cantaloupe samples. Although famous for its cantaloupes, which many think have a status comparable to that of the famous Maine lobsters, local farmers also brag about the more than one million bulbs of the large onions known as onion blossoms.

Adventures in History

Pecos earned bragging rights to the "world's first rodeo" title back in 1883 on July 4. The story begins with a contest to judge the best roper and ends with the winners receiving some money and a few blue ribbons. In an article, Danny Freeman of the Sharlot Hall Museum and author of *The World's Oldest Rodeo 100-Year History 1888–1988* writes of the dispute to the title by the town of Prescott, Arizona. The first Cowboy Tournament in Prescott in 1888 is the town's claim to fame, and the Prescott Frontier

Days Committee applied to the U.S. Patent Office for the rights to "World's Oldest Rodeo." Threats of lawsuits loomed when the makers of the game Trivial Pursuit identified Prescott with the first rodeo with its question "What rough and tumble sport first formalized in Prescott, Arizona?" After researching, the game company continued to lay the title at Prescott's feet, but the town of Pecos continues its claim of being the "Home of the World's First Rodeo" and continues to celebrate the tradition every July 4th with its annual West of the Pecos Rodeo.

The annual rodeo, a weeklong celebration, draws more than one hundred cowboys, including world-class rodeo champions, to vie for the prize money. The prize purse in 2003 climbed to $203,000. Rodeo events include bull riding, team roping, wild horse race, steer wrestling, calf wrestling, barrel racing, and wild cow milking. Weeklong events include Night in Old Pecos, the Cantaloupe Festival, a rodeo dance, the Old-Timers Reunion, and West of the Pecos Rodeo Parade.

The West of the Pecos Museum is housed in the old Orient Hotel, once the finest in the region with fifty rooms. In 2004 the museum, an internationally recognized historic landmark, celebrated the hotel's one hundredth anniversary. The museum is filled with artifacts, history, and West Texas lore. Exhibits include a replica of Judge Roy Bean's Jersey Lilly Saloon. With a Pecos Bill Room, a Bunkhouse, a Rodeo Room, and the Law West of the Pecos Room, the museum provides a glimpse into the full range of history in the area.

On the Map

Pecos is in far West Texas at the intersection of Interstate 20, U.S. 285, and Texas 17.

Weekend Adventures

The 1937 Reeves County Courthouse replaced the original courthouse built in 1886. Be sure to stop by the tombstone of the Gentleman

Gunfighter, Clay Allison, in downtown Pecos behind the bullet-riddled Orient Hotel. Although Allison may have died with his proverbial boots on, his head was crushed by a wagon. The Old Depot and Caboose, Judge Roy Bean's Jersey Lilly Saloon Replica, and Old #11 Saloon bring back those wild Pecos days. Nearby are the MacDonald Observatory, Fort Davis National Historic Site, the Overland Trail Museum, the Rattlesnake Bomber Base, and the strange lights in Marfa.

BEST TIME TO VISIT

The annual July 4th West of the Pecos Rodeo attracts thousands of participants and visitors. Ranked the fourth largest in Texas, the rodeo boasts a large purse of more than $200,000 and is often called the Cowboy Christmas. June is cantaloupe time with the Night in Old Pecos/Cantaloupe Festival and the annual Golden Girl of the Old West Revue and the Little Miss Cantaloupe of the Old West Pageant.

ADVENTURES IN LODGING AND DINING

In Pecos, try the Quality Inn or Best Western Swiss Clock Inn. Once known as the 1883 historic Lempert Hotel, the Veranda Bed and Breakfast & Country Inn, located in Fort Davis, claims to be the oldest Texas establishment of its kind west of the Pecos and one of the oldest in the state. If you're in cattle country, then go for a good steak and try the Cattleman's Restaurant, Sandra's Tejano Steakhouse, or the Alpine Lodge Restaurant. To prove everything's big in Texas, Mrs. Wilson's Texas Sized Doughnuts boasts a doughnut nearly half a foot in diameter. The La Norteña Tortilla Factory offers a wide variety of Mexican food, but the tamales continue to be their main item.

FOR MORE INFORMATION

Contact the Pecos Area Chamber of Commerce and Convention and Visitor's Bureau (www.pecostx.com).

THE KING OF WESTERN SWING: TURKEY'S FAVORITE SON

TURKEY

The discovery of wild turkeys along a creek gave birth to the settlement known as Turkey Roost, but over time the town simply became known as Turkey. Because it sits at the bottom of the Cap Rock near Caprock Canyons State Park, some call Turkey the dead end of tornado alley. Storms roll, rain pelts, and thunder echoes off the canyon creating a natural symphony, but that's not the only music heard in the land of wild turkeys where the bison now roam.

ADVENTURES IN HISTORY

Eight-year-old fiddler Bob Wills moved to Turkey in 1913 and went on to become the King of Western Swing and Turkey's favorite son. Known to sit on the curb outside the barbershop, Bob fiddled away and played his first dance at the age of ten. For the next fourteen years, he played his fiddle music for the many ranch dances held in West Texas. During that time, he learned blues and jazz from black children he played with and later black coworkers. Over time, folks said Wills somehow managed to combine the music of the fiddle with the heat of blues to create something that had the swing of jazz. Whatever it was, his music became known as Western Swing.

Wills left Turkey in 1929 and headed for Fort Worth. A traveling medicine show hired him as a blackface minstrel. He then performed on radio shows, organized the band Lightcrust Doughboys, and even worked for the future governor of Texas, W. Lee O'Daniel. He later moved to Oklahoma and started a new band, the Texas Playboys. When his song, "New San Antonio Rose," became popular, Wills achieved national status and headed for Hollywood. He made nineteen movies. After being elected to the Country Music Hall of Fame, Wills was honored by the state of Texas for his unique contribution to American music as the creator of Western Swing. Still going strong in 1973, Wills and his Texas Playboys received a Grammy for his last album "For the Last Time: Bob Wills and His Texas Playboys." He died on May 13, 1975, and is buried in Memorial Park in Tulsa, Oklahoma.

The story doesn't end there. Wills has been inducted into the Country Music Hall of Fame in Nashville, and he is the only performer, other than Gene Autry, to have also been voted into the National Cowboy Hall of Fame in Oklahoma, City. Today Turkey remembers Bob Wills and continues to celebrate his life with a monument at the west end of Main Street, the Bob Wills Museum, and a week dedicated to the King of Western Swing. Crowds of ten to fifteen thousand stream into the small community to celebrate Bob Wills, his music, and his memory, with the grand reunion topped off with Bob Wills Day on the last Saturday in April. With a parade, a barbecue, concerts, and nightly dances, the small town reverberates with the sound of Western Swing. Fiddles sing, and fans enjoy the Old Fiddlers Contest and the new generation of fiddle bands. The old Assembly of God church is now the Church of Western Swing, complete with a stage, Bob Wills's posters and memorabilia and plenty of old-time jam sessions during Bob Wills week. Although the church rocks with music, don't plan to smoke or drink.

On the Map

Turkey, a West Texas town located fifteen miles from Caprock Canyons State Park, sits at the intersection of State Highways 86 and 70. The town is 100 miles southeast of Amarillo, 100 miles northeast of Lubbock, and 250 miles northwest of Dallas. Try the scenic route to Interstates 40 and 27.

Weekend Adventures

For a trip into yesteryear, check out Lacy's Dry Goods, an old-fashioned dry goods store owned and operated by the Lacy family for more than seventy-five years. For entertainment, try the Midway Drive-in or the GEM Theater. For a bit of history, you have to stop by the Bob Wills Museum and the Turkey Roost Museum. If you have time, visit Caprock Canyons State Park and Caprock Canyons Trailway in nearby Quitaque—fifteen miles from Turkey—and explore one of the best kept secrets in the Panhandle. In addition to having landscape and wildlife that would make a jaded photographer grab his camera, the park offers day-use and camping facilities, hiking, horseback riding, mountain bike riding, a scenic drive, guided tours, and seasonal concessions offering horse rentals. April, May, September, and October offer Canyon Rambles, guided tours from the convenience of open-air vehicles. If you go, check the weather report as the temperatures can start in the 60s in the morning only to reach the high 90s hours later, and be sure to take plenty of water. Thunderstorms develop quickly, too. If you'd rather take a tour by van or bus, contact Queen of the Valley Tours.

BEST TIME TO VISIT

The annual event held on the last Saturday in April, actually a two-day event, called Bob Wills Day rates the highest for music and wall-to-wall food and fun.

ADVENTURES IN LODGING AND DINING

The historical Hotel Turkey, built in 1927, is listed with the State and National Historic Registries. The hotel, run as a bed and breakfast, has remained in continuous operation since 1927 and retains its original décor in all fifteen rooms. Dining is offered at Hotel Turkey. Galvan's Restaurant on Main Street offers authentic Mexican food and American favorites.

FOR MORE INFORMATION

Go to the town's website, www.turkeytexas.com. For information on Bob Wills Day, Bob Wills Museum, or the Bob Wills Foundation, contact the President of the Bob Wills Foundation, P.O. Box 306, Turkey, TX 79261 (806-423-1291 or 806-423-1033).

Appendix
Texas Fairs and Festivals

——— JANUARY ———

The Southwestern Exposition and Stock Show—Fort Worth

——— FEBRUARY———

George Washington Birthday Celebration—Laredo
Great Country River Festival—San Antonio
Mardi Gras—Galveston
San Antonio Livestock Show and Rodeo—San Antonio
The Southwestern Exposition and Stock Show—Fort Worth

——— MARCH ———

Annual Reenactment at the Presidio Living History Weekend—Goliad
Annual General Granbury Birthday Celebration and Bean and
Houston Livestock Show & Rodeo—Houston
Nacogdoches Azalea Trails—Nacogdoches
St. Patrick's Day Festival—Dublin
Rib Cook Off—Granbury
Tablerock Festival—Salado

Texas Cowboy Poetry Gathering—Alpine
Texas Dogwood Trails Celebration—Palestine

———— APRIL ————

Billy the Kid Day—Hico
Blue Grass Festival—Glen Rose
Bob Wills Day—Turkey
Brazos River Festival—Waco
Cotton Palace Pageant—Waco
Dawn of the Alamo/Remember the Alamo—San Antonio
El Paso Heritage Festival—Fort Bliss
Fair on the Square Annual Street Dance—Rusk
Fiesta En La Calle—Yorktown
Fiesta San Antonio—San Antonio
Fort Selden Frontier Days—Fort Bliss
Great Race of Texas—Granbury
Historic Homes Tour—Gonzales
Historic Homes Tour—Victoria
Houston International Festival—Houston
Jim Reeves Jamboree—Carthage
Lubbock Arts Festival—Lubbock
Mesquite Championship Rodeo—Mesquite (April–September)
Nacogdoches Azalea Trails—Nacogdoches
Old South Festival—Liendo Plantation, Hempstead
Poteet Strawberry Festival—Poteet
San Jacinto Day & Reenactment—San Jacinto
Battleground Complex
Stephens County's Frontier Days—Breckenridge
Texas Dogwood Trails Celebration—Palestine
Wildflower Art Show—Salado
Wildflower Trails of Texas Festival—Linden

—— MAY ——

Big Bend Hall of Fame Cowboy Rendezvous—Marfa
Cinco de Mayo Celebration—Goliad
Cinco de Mayo—San Antonio
Fair on the Square & the Annual Street Dance—Rusk
Fredericksburg Founders Festival—Fredericksburg
Frontier Days—Breckenridge
Maifest—Brenham
Monroe's Bluegrass Festival—Texarkana
O. Henry Pun-Off World Championships—Austin
Stephens County's Frontier Days—Breckenridge
Western Heritage Classic—Abilene

—— JUNE ——

Bach Festival—Victoria
Celebration of President George H. W. Bush and First Lady Barbara
Bush Birthdays—George Bush Presidential Library, College Station
Dr Pepper Week—Dublin
Juneteenth Celebration—Lubbock
Juneteenth Emancipation Celebration
Juneteenth Emancipation Trail Ride—Galveston
Night in Old Pecos/Cantaloupe Festival—Pecos
Texas Blueberry Festival—Nacogdoches
Texas Folklife Festival—San Antonio

—— JULY ——

Americana Jam—Smooth Water Ranch, Hico
Arts & Crafts Festival—Granbury
Chisholm Trail Roundup—Fort Worth

Fourth of July Celebration—Hempstead
Fourth of July Parade—Granbury
Fourth of July West of the Pecos Rodeo—Pecos
Great Texas Mosquito Festival—Clute
Old Settlers Reunion—Hico
Sparks in the Park—Texarkana
Texas International Apple Festival—Bandera
Watermelon Festival—Hempstead
Yorktown Independence Day Celebration—Yorktown

——— AUGUST ———

August Art Fair—Salado
Festival Folklife Festival—San Antonio
John Rex Reeves Pickin' Party—Carthage
Remax Ballunar Liftoff—Houston (NASA)
Texas Country Music Hall of Fame Awards
Ceremony & Show—Carthage

——— SEPTEMBER ———

American Music Festival—Nacogdoches
Four State Fair & Rodeo—Texarkana
Marfa Lights Festival—Marfa
Monroe's Bluegrass Festival—Texarkana
National Cowboy Symposium and Celebration—Lubbock
Panhandle–South Plains Fair—Lubbock
Pioneer Days—Fort Worth
O. Henry Birthday Celebration—Austin
Quadrangle Festival—Texarkana
Sherman Arts Festival—Sherman
State Fair of Texas—Dallas

Tri-State Fair—Amarillo
West Texas Fair & Rodeo—Abilene

OCTOBER

Annual Tour de Goliad Bike Ride—Goliad
Blue Grass Festival—Glen Rose
Chinati Arts Foundation Open House—Marfa
Come and Take It Celebration—Gonzales
Harvest Moon Arts & Crafts Festival—Granbury
Indian Summer Arts & Craft Fair—Rusk
50s Fun Day—Breckenridge
Guadalupe County Fair & Rodeo—Seguin
Matagorda Day—Matagorda
Music Festival—Breckenridge
Pioneer Festival—Rusk
Pumpkin Patch Party—Breckenridge
Red Steagall Cowboy Gathering and Western
Swing Festival—Fort Worth
State Fair of Texas—Dallas
Turkeyfest—Cuero
Yorktown Western Days—Yorktown

NOVEMBER

Civil War Weekend—Hempstead
Nine Flags Festival—Nacogdoches
Pecan Fest—Seguin

DECEMBER

Candlelight Tours—Granbury
Dickens on the Strand—Galveston

Festival of Lights—Hempstead
Festival of Lights—San Antonio
Freeport Audubon Christmas Bird Count—Freeport
Heritage Tour Homes—Seguin
Holiday River Parade and Lighting Ceremony—San Antonio
Nine Flags Festival—Nacogdoches

Index